# *mbaMission*
## *Complete Start-to-Finish*
## *MBA Admissions Guide*

● ● ● ● ● ● ● ● ● ● ● ● ● ● ● ● ● ●

### by Jeremy Shinewald

MGPrep Publishing • New York

**mbaMission Complete Start-to-Finish MBA Admissions Guide**

Published by MGPrep Publishing, Inc
138 W 25th St, 7th Floor
New York, NY 10001
www.mgprep.com

Copyright © 2010 by MGPrep Publishing, Inc., New York, NY

ISBN: 978-1-935707-00-4

Manufactured in the United States of America

Layout Design by Dan McNaney and Cathy Huang

Cover Design by Evyn Williams

*To Seamane Flanagan, writer, editor, collaborator extraordinaire, who made this book possible and probably, ultimately, even edited this very line.*

# About mbaMission

Since Ambassadorial Speechwriter and MBA Jeremy Shinewald founded mbaMission in 1999, we have worked closely with business school candidates from around the world, successfully guiding them through the entire admissions process ("from start to finish") and ensuring that each of their unique attributes is showcased in a creative, compelling, and focused way. We are published authors with elite MBA experience who work one-on-one with clients to discover, select, and articulate the unique stories that will force admissions committees to take notice. We work on all aspects of the application process, helping to reduce candidates' stress levels and maximize applicants' chances of gaining admission to top American and international business schools.

*mbaMission offers all candidates a free half-hour consultation (www.mbamission.com/ consult.php).*

# About the Author

Before founding mbaMission, **JEREMY SHINEWALD** was chief speechwriter for the Ambassador of Israel to the United States, for whom he wrote more than 70 policy addresses. As his speeches were being published in the *Washington Post, Washington Times,* and other major international media outlets, Jeremy was also laying the foundation for mbaMission, helping a small number of applicants gain acceptance to top-tier MBA programs each year. Jeremy was admitted to several top domestic and international MBA programs himself and ultimately became one of the youngest members of his class at the University of Virginia's Darden School of Business, where he was an admissions interviewer, wrote a Business Ethics case and a Small Business Acquisitions case, and was chosen by his peers to be Class Graduation Speaker. After graduation, Jeremy formally established mbaMission and has subsequently provided admissions consulting services to applicants from the United States and more than 25 other countries on six continents. Jeremy is a member of the Board of Directors of the Association of International Graduate Admissions Consultants, an organization committed to upholding the highest standards of ethical practice in MBA advisory services.

# mbaMission Contributors

*Several of mbaMission's top consultants contributed to this publication. Here are just a few of the members of our incredible team.*

While studying Philosophy at Yale, ANGELA GUIDO managed the *Yale Record*, the nation's oldest college humor magazine. Upon graduating, she moved to South Korea, where, in addition to writing for multiple local publications, she taught English as a second language and later coordinated writing and communications training programs at KPMG Korea. Angela joined the Boston Consulting Group (BCG) after completing her MBA at the University of Chicago, where she was named a Siebel Scholar and served on the Dean's Student Admissions Committee. During her two years as a consultant at BCG, Angela participated in writing *Treasure Hunt: Inside the Mind of the New Consumer*, a bestselling book by Michael Silverstein. Angela later served as Women's Initiative Captain and Recruiting Manager for BCG. In that role, she reviewed resumes, conducted case interview preparation sessions, and led workshops for hundreds of candidates to help them better tell their personal stories in interviews.

While earning her MBA from Harvard Business School (HBS), MONICA OKRAH was a Board Member of Harbus News Corporation and collaborated on *65 Successful Harvard Business School Application Essays*—a collection of essays and critiques that showcase the broad range of writing styles and creative content found in successful HBS applications. Before attending HBS, Monica was an Associate at Rice Financial Products Company, an innovative derivatives boutique in New York City, as well as an Investment Banking Analyst at JPMorgan Securities. Monica was also part of a start-up team at Red Ventures, an Internet marketing firm. Monica is an active member and former Chief Marketing Officer of the HBS Alumni Club of Charlotte, North Carolina.

Having been admitted to several top domestic business schools and even earning a fellowship elsewhere, **ERIN FOLEY SCHUHMACHER** ultimately chose to attend HBS. There Erin worked on an independent study for a national retail franchise and served as an Ambassador for the admissions committee—hosting prospectives, leading campus-wide information sessions and participating in Q&A conference calls for newly admitted students. Before attending business school, Erin was a Research Associate for Donaldson, Lufkin and Jenrette and Banc of America Securities, where she authored and edited white papers on the retail industry. Most recently, Erin worked at Financial Risk Management, a London-based fund of hedge funds company, performing due diligence on investments and producing qualitative research reports. Erin currently volunteers with Upwardly Global, a nonprofit organization devoted to assisting legal, professionally trained immigrants in their job search process, and tutors inmates at Bayview Women's Correctional Facility through the New York Junior League.

After earning her MBA with distinction from HBS, **JESSICA SHKLAR** worked at several Fortune 100 companies, including American Express and JPMorgan Chase, where she was the Quality Leader and a Senior Vice President for Chase Home Finance. Jessica is also a Six Sigma Master Black Belt, with specific expertise in Six Sigma deployment and initialization. She earned a degree in Anthropology from Harvard College, and was later Admissions Advisor at a small university in Los Angeles, where she worked closely with undergraduate, business school and other graduate school applicants throughout the admissions process. Jessica also developed and ran workshops for students across the country on how to write effective application essays and has written admissions materials, marketing brochures and several admissions-related articles.

After graduating from Harvard College, **AKIBA SMITH-FRANCIS** became a Management Consultant with McKinsey & Company, where her work focused primarily on the firm's Nonprofit Practice. She later received a joint MBA/MPA from HBS and the Kennedy School of Government. She has contributed articles on finance for *Moxy Magazine*, a magazine for young professional women, and is one of the founding members of the Board of Directors of Cool Kids Learn, Inc., which provides academic enrichment programs that help children build the love of learning they need to succeed in school and in life. She was also a founding member of the Smith Leadership Academy (no relation), a charter school in Boston. She is currently writing a book tentatively titled *Stepping Off the Path*, an anthology of advice and vignettes from people who left conventional careers to pursue their true callings.

The following *mbaMission Insider's Guides* are also available from mbaMission (online at www.mbamission.com/store.php), and more are being added regularly:

Columbia Business School

Duke University's Fuqua School of Business

Harvard Business School

Kellogg School of Management

MIT Sloan School of Management

New York University Stern School of Business

Stanford Graduate School of Business

Tuck School of Business

UC-Berkeley Haas School of Business

UCLA Anderson School of Management

University of Chicago Booth School of Business

University of Michigan Ross School of Business

University of Virginia Darden School of Business Administration

Wharton School of the University of Pennsylvania

# TABLE OF CONTENTS

| 13 | Introduction |
| 17 | 1. Long-Term Planning |
| 53 | 2. Brainstorming |
| 63 | 3. Essay Writing |
| 105 | 4. Resume |
| 131 | 5. Personal Statement |
| 163 | 6. Letters of Recommendation |
| 185 | 7. Optional Essays |
| 207 | 8. Interview |
| 231 | 9. Waitlist |
| 247 | 10. Closing Thoughts |

# *mbaMission Complete*
# *Start-to-Finish*
## *MBA Admissions Guide*

# Introduction

# *Introduction*

After more than a decade of helping hundreds of MBA applicants get into top American and international business schools, we have learned a thing or two about what it takes to compel an admissions committee to send that coveted letter of acceptance. While we always work closely and meticulously with our clients to ensure their unique stories and qualities shine through in their applications, some of our advice boils down to key fundamentals: approach each essay with a brainstorming session, draft an outline, make personal statements truly personal, tailor your resume to the admissions committee's needs, approach your recommenders strategically and prepare extensively for your interviews. Now, via this book, we offer you our thoughts on these subjects so that you too can begin your journey toward the MBA of your dreams.

Many applicants are terrified at the prospect of applying to business school, and some approach the application process in a haphazard and ill-advised manner. As a result, the process often becomes extremely stressful, and results can be disappointing. We truly believe that with some basic organization, a simple strategy and helpful professional guidance, applying to business school can actually be enjoyable and rewarding, not to mention successful!

We encourage you to visit our Web site, www.mbamission.com, which includes complete and detailed analysis of all the top American and international business schools' essay questions, as well as a free weekly essay-writing tip. Explore our blog frequently, as we are constantly updating it and adding new free resources.

Of course, the information in this guide and the analysis and tips on our site are no substitute for working with a dedicated mbaMission professional. Each MBA candidate is unique. We all have distinct personal stories to tell, and we all face challenges in telling them. mbaMission consultants are specifically trained to ensure that you tell your stories in the most interesting and compelling way—and that you take advantage of even the tiniest opportunity that might help you gain admission to your ideal MBA program.

We hope you enjoy this book. If you need any advice at all with respect to any element of applying to business school, please feel free to contact us for a free consultation.

**Jeremy Shinewald**
*info@mbamission.com*
*www.mbamission.com*
*646-485-8844*
*Skype: mbaMission*

## mbaMission

Visit our resource page: http://www.mbamission.com/resources.php.

You will find links to FREE mbaMission materials:

- Personal statement guide
- Brainstorming questions in a workable word format
- Resume templates in a workable word format
- mbaMission admissions webinars
- More…

# Long-Term Planning

## Chapter 1

# The Big Picture: Planning and Executing Your Business School Application

As you contemplate your long-term MBA plan, several questions will no doubt arise: "Are my grades good enough? What is a safe GMAT score? How much work experience will I need? Who should recommend me? Am I a well-rounded candidate?"

Before you begin working on your applications, understanding how competitive you are as a candidate is crucial. By considering this issue well in advance of your application year, you will be able to plan out the steps you need to take to become a competitive candidate, reduce your potential for disappointment and simplify the task of applying to business school. In the first part of this chapter, we will introduce you to the main aspects of your candidacy that the admissions committees will be evaluating. In the second part of this chapter, we will guide you along your journey by providing a one-year planning timeline to help you manage the process, ensuring that you maximize all possible opportunities along the way to enhance your candidacy. Many candidates will embark on this journey about one year before they plan to submit their completed application, but you can certainly adjust your calendar to fit your plans and get started even earlier.

Although we offer these practical steps, remember that no set "recipe" exists for gaining admission to a top MBA program. Your individuality is your greatest asset, and your personal/professional story will be crucial as you strive to differentiate yourself among an ultracompetitive pool.

Long-Term Planning

# Your Application from the Admissions Committee's Perspective

## Your Numbers

Questions you might have:

- *What is a good GPA and a strong GMAT score?*

- *How much do these numbers matter?*

- *What should I do if my scores are low?*

- *What if I have not taken any business, finance or math classes since high school?*

The admissions committee's question:

- *Can you handle the work?*

When admissions committees examine your "numbers," they ask themselves whether you will be able to handle their rigorously analytical and highly quantitative MBA program. Your GMAT score and grades will be the foremost indicator of your strengths in these areas, with the GMAT holding more sway the more time has passed since your college graduation. However, no particular set or level of scores will guarantee that you will get into a top school—some schools even brag about the number of 780s (considered a whopping GMAT score) they reject each year. The MBA admissions process is holistic, and all the aspects of your profile will be evaluated.

There is no hard and fast rule about what grades and scores are "good enough" for any given program. We recommend researching published statistics on average and median GPAs and GMAT scores at the school(s) you are targeting. For reference, the average total GMAT score at schools that are generally considered to be the top 15 programs (according to the Bloomberg *BusinessWeek* and *U.S. News & World Report* rankings) is about 710. If you are applying to one of these schools, you should aim for that score or higher. You should also strive for a balanced score, achieving an 80th percentile or higher on both sections of the GMAT (verbal and quantitative). In particular, an 80th percentile on the quantitative portion[1] will clearly indicate to the admissions committee that you can handle the difficult analytical work required in the MBA curriculum.

If you do not score 710 or higher, however, fear not! This is just the *average* score, which means that a good percentage of the previous class of admitted students scored below that—not everyone can be above average!

We recommend the following ways to help ensure you attain the best GMAT score possible before submitting your application:

- *Study for the test:* This advice may seem obvious to some, but many candidates do not fully understand that the GMAT is not a test that you can simply take "cold." In fact, our friends at Kaplan GMAT inform us that to truly be well prepared for the exam, candidates should dedicate a minimum of 100 hours to studying—two to three months of combined classroom and self-guided practice. These days, many test-prep options are available beyond the traditional classroom experience, including pure self-study with score-qualified advanced courses, live online classes, on-demand classes, and private tutoring. A number of free resources are available from Kaplan GMAT on their facebook (http://www.facebook.com/kaplanGMAT) and twitter pages (http://www.twitter.com/KaplanGMATPrep) and we recommend taking advantage of them, particularly the free practice tests and sample classes.

Long-Term Planning

---

1   It is worth noting that achieving an 80th percentile score on the quantitative section of the GMAT is becoming increasingly difficult, as scores continue to rise. Thus, some schools have begun to note that a 75 percentile score is a "safe" target.

- *Take the test sooner rather than later:* Many candidates do not realize that they can take the GMAT up to five years in advance of submitting their application. Admissions offices generally prefer test scores from the previous three years, but our point is that you should not feel that you must take the test only during the year in which you apply. Further, by taking the test earlier, you leave yourself sufficient time to take the test again (you can take the test only once per month) if you do not score as well as you had hoped. You may be surprised to know that admissions committees actually encourage candidates to take the test multiple times—they want you to do your best, and higher average GMAT scores, which factor into MBA rankings, can help to boost a school's position. By taking the GMAT early, you will also free up time closer to the application deadline to dedicate to other aspects of applying to business school.

Your GMAT score will be especially important if you graduated from college more than five years ago or if your undergraduate GPA was below the average for students at your target school(s) (approximately 3.5 for the top MBA programs noted earlier). Although we recommend making every effort to achieve the best score you possibly can, you should take care not to focus on your GMAT to the exclusion of all else.

Admissions committees consider your GPA another important indicator of your ability to succeed in the challenging academic environment of an MBA classroom. But as with your GMAT score, there is no "right" GPA. In evaluating your transcript, admissions committees will take into account your grades, your major, the institution you attended (though to a lesser degree), any trends over time (e.g., did you get all As toward the end of college that offset a few early Cs?) and the nature and rigor of your course of study. In particular, they will look for evidence of some quantitative horsepower. If your transcript does not include any management, economics, finance or math classes that prove you have done well in quantitative subjects in the past, you will need to find another way to prove your competencies in these areas. Fortunately, doing so is definitely possible. For example, if nothing on your transcript or in your work history indicates your ability to manage the quantitative work required by an MBA program, you can build up what is referred to in the admissions world as an "alternate transcript" before you apply by taking two courses at a local college in any of the following areas: accounting, finance, economics, statistics and calculus. Whichever subject you choose, you will need to do well for the course to reflect positively on your candidacy—a B+ is acceptable, but an A is far better if you are trying to prove that you can compete amid a quantitatively strong peer group at the MBA level. Alternatively, you might consider completing Level I of the Chartered Financial Analyst (CFA) designation, which would reveal that you have the maturity and drive to dedicate yourself to a rigorous self-guided study program and that you have strong pre-MBA knowledge of the academic areas noted earlier. (Note: the CFA program can be remarkably time-consuming, and we recommend completing Level I well in advance of your application year.)

Although your GPA and your GMAT score are important, high scores do not guarantee success in the application process, and low scores do not guarantee failure. We have seen candidates with 540 GMAT scores get into Harvard and applicants with 780s fail to do so. Our point? The admissions committees will examine your profile **holistically**, attempting to appropriately gauge your qualities as both an individual and a professional, plus your potential to contribute to your class and to achieve in your career. Stats are only one factor in their broader decision.

Long-Term Planning

# Your Goals

Questions you might have:

- *What kinds of goals are the right goals to have?*

- *How specific is specific enough?*

The admissions committee's questions:

- *Will the program really be of value to you?*

- *Will you make the school proud as an alumnus/alumna?*

Defining post-MBA goals is difficult for many candidates. Most people applying to business school recognize that the degree will pay dividends beyond what they can anticipate, open doors in their career regardless of the direction they choose and provide an education that will be valuable in most business endeavors. Should that not be justification enough for seeking an MBA? Others pursue MBA studies to diversify their skills and discover new professional avenues. Should that not be encouraged?

Perhaps those reasons are sufficient for you, but consider the issue from the admissions committees' perspective. By offering you one of the very few, highly sought-after places in their program, they are essentially investing in you. They therefore want to know what you plan to do with that investment. Their goal is to provide value and create happy, successful alumni. They will look at your goals and aspirations to understand whether an MBA from their program will indeed further your goals and be of value to you—your ultimate success will reflect well on the school. For most schools, wanting an MBA just for the education is not enough. You have to have a plan for your—and their—investment.

Fortunately, there are no right or wrong career goals for a business school candidate, only more or less well thought-out ones. If you have a broad sense of what you want to do—maybe you have an industry in mind—but are not sure of your specific plan, we recommend doing some honest exploration of your goals well before you begin to apply. Perhaps, for example, you believe you want to work in finance in general but are unsure of what lies behind the buzzwords "investment banking," "sales and trading," "asset management" and "equity research." In this case, take the time to do some research and explore the post-MBA opportunities that exist (a good way to generate career ideas is to visit different schools' career services Web sites) and then take action to gain some a priori experience in your potential field or in the function that appeals to you via informational interviews and job shadowing. Understanding *how* an MBA will be useful in the area you are considering is key to effectively conveying your need for the degree to the admissions committees.

We recommend that when you discuss your goals in your essays, you be as detailed as you can credibly be without stretching your believability. (See our Personal Statement chapter for examples of the appropriate level of detail.) If the thought of committing yourself to a path now is daunting, do not worry. Admissions committees understand that people change their minds, especially as they learn more and are exposed to new options and information as part of the MBA experience. (No one will force you at graduation to adhere to the goals you present in your application!) You should keep in mind that an MBA is a significant investment of your time and money. So, if you are not sure that you will use the degree to further yourself in your career, it may not be worth your time and energy to pursue such an intense program. So dig deep, do some soul-searching and be sure to develop goals that really inspire you.

Long-Term Planning

# Your Professional Life

Questions you might have*:*

- *What is the right kind of experience?*

- *What if I have never managed a team?*

- *Do I have enough experience?*

The admissions committee's question*:*

- *Will you contribute meaningfully to the class/business school community?*

In addition to their desire to turn out successful leaders, business schools want to be sure that the candidates they admit will be able to participate meaningfully in the MBA classroom and bring a perspective to class discussions that will be valuable to their classmates. Your career trajectory and professional accomplishments (revealed through your resume, essays, recommendations and interviews) will be a strong indicator of your ability both to contribute to the class and to be a leader beyond.

As with some of the other elements of your candidacy that we have discussed thus far, no set rule is in place as to the "right" amount or type of work experience, nor is there a "right" career trajectory. Each year we hear from a few candidates who fear that their professional position is a liability: "I am a school teacher. Maybe if I transitioned to consulting, I would get into the school of my dreams." Although bankers and consultants are certainly well represented at top business schools and teachers are not, this is not evidence of a bias among admissions officers, but instead of the nature of these workplaces. Most bankers and consultants need an MBA to progress past a certain point on the corporate ladder, whereas no teacher truly *needs* an MBA to progress.

What is more important than targeting a particular industry or position for the future is conveying your performance in past endeavors. Places are available in the MBA classes at all top schools for high-performing teachers, consultants and bankers alike—but not for low-performing individuals in any field. The leading business school programs want a diversity of experience in their classrooms, and they want candidates who exhibit the promise of achievement—not just a job title—going forward.

The admissions committees will examine your professional experiences to see whether you tend to take on increasing responsibility in your work. This may be evidenced by promotions or by simply having more impact on the bottom line of your department or company through informal influence (without a promotion). After all, the lowest man on the totem pole can have the greatest influence in a project's outcome if he is willing to speak up and get buy-in for his ideas.

The admissions committees are also interested in the kind of impact you have had on others, in either formal or informal ways, such as direct management, mentorship or training roles. If you have never managed another employee or a team, do not worry. Many candidates applying to business school are in the same position. Leadership and management are actually two different things, and admissions committees take both into account. Whereas management entails directly supervising other employees, leadership can include such broad interpersonal activities as mentorship, training, coaching, influencing and persuading others to adopt your ideas, taking responsibility for an outcome, helping a floundering teammate and creating open and productive communication within a team. More simply, for our purposes, management is the use of position to gain the best outcomes and leadership is the use of persuasion to gain the best outcomes. Examine your personal and professional history for these kinds of examples, and if examples are lacking, start looking now for opportunities to contribute to others and to take responsibility for the outcome of your work, so you will be able to discuss these in your application. If your job provides an insufficient outlet

Long-Term Planning

for leadership, seek opportunities to lead in your extracurricular and community service activities.

At most top programs, students have an average of five to six years of work experience, but we remind you that an average derives from a wide range, meaning that some applicants will be above this figure and some will be below. Every year, candidates with varying degrees of experience gain admission to business school, and having more or less is neither "good" nor "bad." The key is what you have been able to accomplish during your work history and the kind of potential this demonstrates for your post-MBA goals. Admissions committees will look beyond your industry, company name, title and years of experience and strive to identify **performance!**

# Community Service and Other Volunteer Contributions

Questions you might have:

- *Do I really need to do community service?*

- *Is it too late to start?*

- *What if I work 8,000 hours a week?*

The admissions committee's question:

- *Are you someone who makes a difference and seeks out challenges?*

Aside from the sincere value that you can bring to your community by volunteering in some way, community work is an important element of your application. From an admissions perspective, contributing to others in this way shows initiative and motivation on your part and can differentiate you from otherwise similar candidates who do not go the extra mile. For example, if you take time outside of work to volunteer with the aged while your peer from work who is also applying to business school instead uses that time to shop or watch TV, all else being equal, you have a distinct advantage. Showing personal commitment to and passion for a cause or organization and seeking leadership opportunities outside of work indicate that you have strong personal qualities and provides the admissions committee with deeper insight into your candidacy.

Still, some applicants mistakenly regard any form of community service as a prerequisite for getting into a top MBA program. These candidates will thus sign up for a volunteer activity without first considering whether it is a reasonable fit for them and/or how their choice could reflect on their candidacy in the admissions committees' eyes. Although community service is a positive, it is not a "one size fits all" element of one's candidacy. As you contemplate your current or potential community involvements, you should recognize that "hours served" are not as important as the spirit of your participation and the extent of your impact.

We therefore encourage MBA candidates to carefully consider their community experiences in the same way they would examine and evaluate their professional or entrepreneurial opportunities. Although people can sometimes make mistakes in their career paths, most gravitate toward areas or opportunities in which they can excel, justifiably to further their own interests. The same is true for volunteer opportunities as well. If, for example, you have always enjoyed a particularly close relationship with your grandmother and want to share this kind of positive experience with others, you might decide to volunteer to spend time with seniors at a retirement home, where you would naturally be predisposed toward success. If you were quite passionate about your work there, you just might get others involved, expand the volunteer program at the home, take greater leadership in the program and more. However, if you are not that passionate about the elderly, but there is a retirement home on your block, no matter how convenient it would therefore be to volunteer, doing so would likely be a mistake for you, because you would lack the spirit of commitment/adventure necessary to ensure that your story materializes and would be compelling to the admissions committee.

Although accomplishments in the community arena can make great subject matter for essays and clearly illustrate that you seek to make a difference, your charitable involvement does not need to be with a registered nonprofit. For example, you can reveal your altruistic spirit through a simple personal commitment to a neighbor, relative or colleague—perhaps by helping them with a weekly chore or serving as a social outlet to someone with limited friends in the area—or perhaps via a small neighborhood beautification initiative or by organizing fitness classes for colleagues or friends. The key is not the organization, but your impact; you must show the admissions committees that you are someone who aspires to excellence, is interested in bettering the lives of others and seeks challenges and opportunities for leadership.

If you have not been involved in a community activity up to now, we can reassure you that it is never too late to start. Again, the admissions committees are interested in your impact and your altruistic spirit and commitment, rather than time served. However, the more time you can commit to such an activity, the more opportunity you will have to truly influence and assist others and the more experiences you will be able to discuss in your essays and interviews. So, starting sooner rather than later is certainly beneficial.

However, perhaps you have had trouble committing to any volunteer activities because you work incredibly long hours. The admissions committees know that such jobs exist, and they will take this into account when evaluating your candidacy. That said, you can always find something to do outside of work to show that you are a well-rounded individual and interested in life. For example, try volunteering at a soup kitchen for a few hours each Sunday; look into online volunteering options; spend some vacation time volunteering internationally. Any effort you devote to a practice or organization outside your work will enhance your profile and give you potentially rich fodder for your essays. We simply recommend finding something in which you are genuinely interested and pursuing that.

# Your Recommendations

Questions you might have:

- *Why are recommendations necessary?*

- *Who should recommend me?*

- *Should they repeat what my essays say?*

The admissions committee's question:

- *What will others say about your accomplishments and character?*

Admissions committees consider recommendations for two key reasons. One, they want to learn about your accomplishments, strengths and weaknesses from a different perspective, and two, they want to understand how another person would assess your character. Your essays will provide them with rich, valuable information about you, and your recommendations will present an objective perspective on who you are.

Most schools ask recommenders very detailed and specific questions. We therefore suggest that you seek letters of recommendation from the people who know you best. Do not make the mistake of thinking that only a recommendation from someone with an impressive title will "count" in the eyes of the admissions committee. The admissions committees hope to gain a deep understanding of your character through your recommendations, and only someone who has worked closely with you will be able to comment vividly on who you are. For example, the CEO of your company may have an impressive resume herself, but if all she knows about you is *your* resume, her answers to questions about your character and unique strengths and weaknesses will fall flat.

Because your recommendations are meant to complement (and not duplicate) your essays and are supposed to be objective, you should not worry if your letters reveal a different side of you or highlight different skills than those you have presented yourself in other parts of your application. In fact, you can benefit from a recommender opening a new window into your character. (See the Letters of Recommendation chapter for detailed tips on preparing your recommenders to write rich and detailed letters on your behalf.)

# Diversity and International Experience

Questions you might have:

- *What if I don't have any international experience?*

- *What kind of experience is the right kind?*

- *Does travel count?*

The admissions committee's question:

- *Can you thrive in a diverse environment?*

These days, admissions officers unquestionably want a geographically and experientially diverse class, and most MBA candidates tend to have had some level of international exposure, either through personal travel or work. Still, admissions committees understand that not all jobs—or lives—provide opportunities for international experience, so if your global exposure is limited at best, you should not be overly concerned, but you will need to consider other ways of illustrating a connection with or interest in other countries and cultures. The ability to deal with diversity is a key challenge for business leaders and MBA students alike, so the admissions committees want to know that you have grappled with some of the issues that diverse environments pose.

Showing an interest in the world through travel is a great start if you have never experienced living or working in a foreign culture. Perhaps you have worked with teams that are ethnically, geographically, generationally or otherwise diverse and have had to address and overcome the communication issues that can arise in such environments. Perhaps through your community service you have come into contact with people whose backgrounds are very different from yours and have succeeded in making a difference for, or profound connection with, those people. Examine your life for any ways in which you have tried to explore and empathize with others' perspectives. If you feel you have not had enough experience with diversity, seek out opportunities to interact meaningfully with people different from you in your community service, extracurricular and work endeavors.

# "Why Our School?"

Questions you might have:

- *How detailed does this need to be?*

- *Do I need to visit the school?*

The admissions committee's questions:

- *Are you sure our program is for you?*

- *Are you a good fit with the program?*

As we have discussed earlier, the admissions committees want to be sure that you are making the right choice for you in applying to their school. MBA programs vary vastly from one to the next in a number of areas, including location, class size/structure, curriculum, pedagogy, academic specializations,

Long-Term Planning

recruitment focus, alumni base, facilities, rankings and reputation. They also differ culturally and experientially. We therefore recommend that you thoroughly research the obvious and subtle differences between programs when choosing the ones you believe are the best fit for you.

When admissions committees are evaluating your discussion of why you have chosen their school (over others), they will first look for evidence that you truly understand their program deeply—beyond the rankings, taglines, marketing mantras and most popular classes. They want to know that you have extensively investigated the school's culture, spoken with students and/ or alumni and really "kicked the tires" of their program to make sure it fits your individual needs and style. To this end, visiting the school and sitting in on a class constitute extremely useful primary research and can also provide compelling stories for you to include in your essays. However, a school visit is generally *not* a prerequisite for admission, and admissions committees will not view your candidacy negatively if you have not been able to visit their school before applying or for your interview (unless you live in the same city as your target school, in which case, they will expect the effort!). We offer several *mbaMission Insider's Guides* for top U.S. MBA programs that will help you jump-start your school research, and even if your target school has not been profiled, reading through another school's guide may give you a good sense of the kind of research you will want to do on your own.

# Application Timing

Questions you might have:

- *Do I need to apply in Round 1?*

- *What if I miss Round 2?*

- *Is applying in Round 3 ever worthwhile?*

The admissions committee's question: *N/A*

Most leading U.S. business schools offer three rounds of admission, and they admit candidates who apply in all three rounds. However, the number/percentage of applicants accepted in each round can vary widely, and each school is different. Applying in the first round rather than in the second or third will not signal a greater commitment to the school to the admissions committee unless the school offers an *early decision* round, in which you agree to pay a hefty deposit if admitted to that school and to withdraw any applications you may have submitted to other schools. If your first-choice school offers early decision and you are sure you would go there if accepted, we recommend going ahead and applying early decision to your target program.

Although the chances of admission are roughly the same between Rounds 1 and 2 at most programs, applying in Round 1 can sometimes offer several advantages. For example, if you plan to apply to more than one school, submitting to one or more programs in the first round will allow you to pace yourself across the first two rounds rather than having all your applications come due at approximately the same time. Moreover, in some cases, you will learn whether you have been admitted to programs to which you applied in the first round before the Round 2 applications are due, which may ultimately save you time and energy you would have otherwise spent on completing additional applications. In addition, if you are admitted in Round 1 to a program you want to attend, you can spend the winter getting to know the school better, preparing for the program and making summer travel plans. And lastly, in the event you are waitlisted first round, the school may reconsider your application in the second (and even third) round, giving you a slightly better overall chance of admission.

If you miss the first round, however, fear not. Although applying in Round 1 confers certain benefits as we just presented, the second round is typically just as good as the first with respect to your chances of gaining admission. Many schools will fill the majority of their incoming class from the second

Long-Term Planning

round, so we recommend submitting your application by the Round 2 deadline. Ideally, if you choose to apply to several schools, we would recommend submitting some in Round 1 and some in Round 2, as mentioned earlier.

As for applying in Round 3, we quote Rose Martinelli, dean of admissions at Chicago Booth: "The truth is that Round 3 can be a bit more competitive simply because the majority of applications and acceptances will occur in Rounds 1 and 2." We do not recommend putting off the application until the third round. By this point, most of the class has been filled, and you will be competing with a very talented pool for only a few open spots. If applying third round is the only option you have, we would encourage you to evaluate your candidacy very carefully, and candidly. If you feel you are truly a standout applicant, you should go ahead and try your luck with a Round 3 application. Even if you are not admitted, the school may look favorably upon your application and urge you to reapply the following year. But our bottom-line advice is to apply on or before the second round deadline, if at all possible.

# *Long-Term Planning Timeline*

Now that we have covered the big picture of your application and given you a sense of what the admissions committee values in your application, we want to provide a step-by-step timeline to help guide you down the long road of applying to business school. The timeline below assumes that you are setting out a year ahead of the deadline. Even if you are starting later, you should be able to leverage this timeline to help you prioritize each step along the way.

## Pre-Stage

The following steps in the application process are somewhat timeless. It is never too soon to take on a leadership position in your community, sign up for a supplemental course, visit your target schools, etc. We have therefore structured this section so that you can consider the steps outlined "ongoing."

## Start Your GMAT Prep

As an aspiring MBA, you don't want to find yourself in a situation where you are juggling many aspects of the application process (GMAT study, essays, class visits, supplementary classes, etc.) at once. So, you should start your GMAT prep as early as possible and thus remove this time-consuming and stressful element of the application process before the bulk of the applications are released in May/June. If you are reading this and truly striving to plan ahead, we strongly recommend that you enroll in a Kaplan GMAT course a full year before you will need to submit your applications/receive decisions. Kaplan GMAT courses are often nine weeks in duration, and you may require a month of additional study afterward to focus on your specific issues. So, if you want to take the GMAT at least once prior to the May/June essay question release dates, you would need to start a class by mid-January. If you want to leave yourself time to take the test more than once (you can only schedule the test once every 31 days up to a maximum of five times each year), you should begin your preparation even earlier.

## Contemplate Additional Coursework/Enroll in Additional Courses

We also recommend that you consider whether you might benefit from some additional coursework, and if so, enroll in classes at an early stage. Was your undergraduate performance weak (i.e., you had a GPA of 3.0 or under)? Did you perform well but take no quantitative coursework at all? If you answered "yes" to either of these questions, you should identify nearby colleges and inquire about their available introductory course offerings in areas such as economics, accounting, finance, calculus and statistics. By taking one or two classes in these areas, you could change the admissions committees' perspective on your academic aptitude.

Long-Term Planning

MBA programs are actually far more forgiving of previous academic problems than other graduate programs are. Most candidates' academic experience is far in the past, and their GMAT score, references and work experience are better indicators of their potential for success. This is not to suggest that poor grades do not matter, but rather, that they can often be mitigated. Of course, it is important that you get As in the courses you take to show that you have an aptitude for that kind of work and also that you take your academics quite seriously. So, enroll now so you will have ample time to complete a semester-long class and have your academic issues "solved"—hopefully by the end of the spring, but by the end of summer at the latest.

## Contemplate School Choices and Visit Target Schools

A surprising number of MBA candidates define their list of target schools by reading popular rankings, such as those produced by *BusinessWeek* and *U.S. News & World Report*. Although rankings can provide a good starting point for your research, we recommend that candidates define specific parameters as to what they consider important in an MBA experience. (For example, would you prefer a case method or lecture environment? A large class or a small class? An urban or small-town campus? A rigid or flexible curriculum?) As you work to define your parameters, you might consider visiting a few campuses to learn about their differences and identify what truly interests you. Most MBA programs open their class visit schedules in October and will facilitate visits into mid-April; again, by scheduling and making these trips early, you will be able to complete—and thus eliminate—this time-consuming aspect of the application process that would otherwise demand your attention as first-round deadlines approach.

Of course, beyond the personal rewards you will gain by visiting a school and taking time to contemplate whether it is an appropriate choice for you, admissions committees generally appreciate when prospective students come to campus, and your visit will better enable you to describe your fit with the school via your essays.

## Accelerate Personal Achievements

By advancing your personal achievements, you can differentiate yourself from the indistinguishable masses. You should immediately consider any personal endeavors that you have started and focus on accelerating the timeline of any achievements that are already within reach. For example, if you have always intended to publish a certain article and have almost completed a final draft, now is the time to finish it. If you have always planned on earning your CFA designation and only have Level III of the exam left, arrange to take the final test this year—don't wait! If you can run 20 miles and have always dreamed of completing a marathon, do it this year. We are not suggesting that if you have never run a mile in your life, you start training for a marathon now; however, if a goal of yours is reasonably in sight and will be otherwise achieved after your applications are due, you should accelerate your timeline to ensure that you have completed it before the first-round deadline.

## Take a Leadership Role in Your Community

In a competitive admissions environment, differentiating yourself from others (almost all of whom will have the ability to showcase their grades, GMAT scores and professional experiences) is important. One way that many candidates reveal more of themselves and their leadership potential to the admissions committees is by taking a leadership role in their communities. You might be thinking to yourself, "But there is so little time left, and the admissions committee will see through my experience!" We recommend that you commit yourself to an organization about which you are passionate as early as possible and strive to make a noticeable impact in the months (or, ideally, longer) before your first-round application deadlines. If you were to start volunteering later in the application season, your gesture would seem far less sincere, and you would lack the profound experiences to explore in your essays. Saying definitely when is "too late" to take such a step is difficult—early is better, but quality of experience trumps quantity.

## Pursue Firm Sponsorship of Your MBA

If you plan to remain with (or return to) your current firm after you receive your MBA, you would be wise to do some research now on whether your firm will sponsor your degree. While the financial benefits of firm sponsorship are obvious, many prospective students do not realize that there is additional power inherent in being a firm-sponsored candidate. The admissions committees know that these applicants, with their firm's backing, will be employed upon graduation and that these individuals' post-MBA goals are thereby "guaranteed." Furthermore, the admissions committee will sleep better knowing that when the school later reports its employment statistics to *Business Week* as part of that publication's regular MBA ranking survey, the program will likely see a small benefit in the "percentage of candidates employed upon graduation" and possibly even "average starting salary" categories.

So, be sure to find out whether your firm has an MBA sponsorship program and, if it does, learn what is necessary to earn a firm scholarship. We at mbaMission have worked with clients who have needed to apply for such a scholarship within their company as long as a year and a half before their proposed MBA programs would begin; obviously, in such cases, you do not want to be applying at the last moment. Similarly, we have worked with clients whose firms did not originally have sponsorship programs, but created them when our candidates brought forth the idea—a process that can involve months of bureaucratic haggling. Consequently, this is certainly a process you should start now.

# February

## Meet with Alumni and Students

As you contemplate your choices and begin visiting campuses, consider augmenting your process of a priori discovery by meeting with your target school's alumni or students, so that you can gain an intimate understanding of these programs. Current students in particular will have an awareness of specific programs and classes that may not be prominently featured on a school's Web site but that may appeal to you and even enable you to strengthen your case for attending that particular school. By meeting with students and alumni and by visiting classes, you will collect a variety of data points that will better equip you to persuade the admissions committee that its school is ideally suited to you, in a way that few others will be able to do.

## Continue with Leadership/Community Work and Continue to Advance Personal Achievements (ongoing)

We will assume that you understand that community leadership and advancing personal achievements should continue on an ongoing basis throughout the admissions season. However, your target schools will not actually be tracking your hours from week to week, so keep in mind that you can dedicate yourself heavily to these activities in the early months of the application season or year and then, as your time demands become more intense in August and September with various application responsibilities, you can shift your focus to other aspects of the application process. Do not forget, though, that you will be judged on the sincerity of your commitment, so you should not scale back your participation so much that your intentions are brought into question.

# March

## Identify Recommenders/Reconnect with Previous Supervisors

We find that one of the most frustrating parts of the application process for candidates is connecting with and motivating recommenders. With some foresight, you can take the time now to identify recommenders (even if you do not approach them for months) and gather some intelligence on each of them. Has your recommender written letters for anyone else? Is he/she generous with his/her time with respect to employee feedback and review sessions? One of the best windows into your recommendation process will be the experiences of any colleagues for whom your target recommenders have already written such a letter; you may want to speak with these individuals to discover how your intended recommender managed their respective processes. By identifying recommenders who will be helpful and generous, you will potentially alleviate the stress of missed deadlines and unpredictable letters.

While you should spend time right now doing your homework on readily available recommenders, you should also take time to reconnect with previous supervisors who could also be strong recommenders, but with whom you have fallen out of touch. You do not want to find yourself in a position where you are calling a former supervisor for the first time in a year or more and asking him/her for a large chunk of time on a tight deadline. If you know you will need to call on a former supervisor, make contact now and keep the relationship warm for the next few months. You will be far better off when the letter-writing process begins. (Note: In most cases, MBA admissions committees have a bias toward current supervisors, but depending on the situation, past supervisors can be acceptable.)

# April

## Take the GMAT for the First Time

Taking the GMAT once by the end of April is ideal, because it allows you to finish one major component of the process just as another—commencing your essays—looms on the horizon. Furthermore, if you take the GMAT in April (or earlier) and do not do as well as you had hoped, you can always retake the exam in May, June or even July if needed. MBA admissions offices often even encourage candidates to take the GMAT more than once. Your scores will not be averaged; instead, schools will, forgivingly, take the higher (or highest) of your scores into consideration.

## Prepare Your Resume

Another simple step you can take now to help reduce competing interests later is prepare your resume and then make small modifications and updates regarding your most recent position in October, in the final stages of the first-round application process. An added benefit is that you will start the process of reflecting on your accomplishments now and reawakening yourself to certain experiences. Preparing your resume now will be a primer for your essay brainstorming process, which will be the foundation for your essays.

# May

## Brainstorm and Start Writing Essays

We at mbaMission always tell our clients, "You can't turn a bad idea into a good essay." We insist on taking our candidates through a lengthy brainstorming process (which begins with a thorough questionnaire) to discover the stories that make each candidate distinct. Even as you uncover your stories, it is still important to consider them from as many different angles as possible. While this will help ensure that you understand the various "weapons in your arsenal," so to speak, this will also provide you with maximum flexibility (considering that MBA admissions committees ask questions that vary dramatically from school to school).

For example, an experience coaching a baseball team at an underfunded high school can actually have multiple dimensions. This may be the story of creatively motivating an underachieving team and changing attitudes, despite losses; of initiating and leading fundraising efforts so that each player can afford proper equipment; of mentoring a struggling player and seeing an improvement in his on-field performance; and more. Your essays will be only as good as your ideas, so do not settle for just the obvious "low-hanging fruit."

Long-Term Planning

## Take the GMAT Again (if necessary)

As noted earlier, the GMAT may not go as well as planned on your first attempt. Not to worry—your first attempt can serve as a dry run and can prepare you for a stronger second attempt. Candidates must wait 31 days before they can retake the GMAT, so if your April test did not give you the results you wanted, a May test would be your next available option. We recommend that if you do need a second shot at the GMAT, you schedule your next session immediately, while the test is still fresh in your mind.

## Informational Interviews/Job Shadow

At mbaMission, we always emphasize that candidates should strive to differentiate themselves from other applicants via their experiences and the sincerity of their voices within their essays. With respect to sincerity, many candidates have trouble honestly articulating their post-MBA goals, and virtually every MBA program requires that candidates write an essay on short- and long-term career goals (HBS being the notable exception; it makes a goal statement optional). If you aspire to enter a competitive field, such as banking or consulting, it may be wise to conduct informational interviews or even to job shadow an individual for a day, if possible. MBA admissions committees frown on vague goal statements or generic claims that lack a profound personal connection to a position and therefore lack credibility. The sincerity of your interest, magnified and thus better articulated as a result of personal experience, can make the difference for you.

# June

## Define List of Target Schools

By mid-June at the latest, most MBA programs will have released their essay questions for the coming year. So, by then, you should have started to pare down your list of target schools and determine which ones you will be applying to in Round 1. Generally, we recommend that MBA aspirants apply to four to six schools, targeting a mix of safe, competitive and reach programs. However, you should never sacrifice quality for quantity—apply only to the number of schools to which you can commit yourself entirely.

## Continue Writing Your Essays (ongoing)

Essay writing takes time and patience. If you are, like the average candidate, trying to complete three to five applications, and you might need to write five or six drafts of four to five essays per school—well, you do the math. You could be writing up to 150 essays within a brief period of time. So, you should be in the thick of your essay writing by June, dedicating a few hours each week to this step and significant time on weekends. You don't need to be a Pulitzer Prize winner to go to business school, but you do need to articulate your vision sincerely and reveal your unique potential through your stories. Needless to write, it is beyond challenging to achieve that in one marathon writing session. Stick with it!

Note: mbaMission offers more than *50 free essay tips* on its Web site.

## Take the GMAT One Last Time (if necessary)

We do not suggest that you take and retake the GMAT forever. However, you will face no penalty for taking the test multiple times. In fact, as we mentioned earlier, most schools are very understanding of multiple attempts, because this shows that you are tenacious. So, if at first you don't succeed and at second you don't succeed, you just might want to try again. Of course, all candidates must use judgment in analyzing their scores and deciding for themselves whether they may be able to do better by retaking the test, but generally, if your scores are consistent after three exams, you should consider moving on and accepting that your score is about as high is it will be (assuming you have truly invested time in studying with the proper resources).

# July

## Meet with Recommenders

In some ways, it is never too early to meet with your recommenders, discuss their important role in the application process and even review your major accomplishments with them, so that these elements remain top-of-mind when they write about you and your achievements. Some candidates may wonder whether such meetings are appropriate. At mbaMission, we not only think that they are appropriate, but also recommend them—as do admissions officers, such as Derrick Bolton, assistant dean and director of admissions at the Stanford Graduate School of Business.

# August

## Complete Additional Coursework

We hope that by August, at the latest, you will have completed your supplemental coursework and earned an A grade (or multiple As). If so, you will have managed to complete another "checked box" and can focus more fully on your essays.

## Complete the Short-Answer Sections

Many candidates will work painstakingly on their essays, prepare rigorously for their interviews and endlessly contemplate their choices of recommenders. However, candidates often leave completing the short-answer sections of their applications (the actual application forms) to the last moment—an approach we don't recommend.

The short-answer sections of business school applications should never be ignored and instead should be completed with the same spirit of diligence that candidates ideally bring to all aspects of their applications. We advise candidates to refrain from pasting bullet points from their resumes in the career section and to contemplate the questions that are asked and write out complete answers in sentence form. (Further, bullets from a resume often lack the necessary context.) While the information conveyed is quite important, we consider the overall message—namely, that candidates are giving care and thought to all aspects of their application—even more crucial.

# September

## Follow Up with Recommenders

Experience has shown that many recommenders will not make writing recommendations a priority and will wait until the last minute to write these letters. Inevitably, many MBA aspirants will wonder, "What if my supervisors don't get their letters done by the deadline?"

In our opinion, the easiest way to ensure that your recommenders complete this task on time is to present them with your own deadline, rather than the school's. If the application to your program of choice is due on October 10th, for example, tell your recommenders that you are submitting on September 30th. By setting this advanced deadline, you can put some mild pressure on your recommender (if he/she misses the fictitious deadline) and not be forced to deal with a major problem (i.e., if this were to have happened on the actual deadline day).

## Seek Feedback

As we have noted, writing standout essays takes time and patience. Still, you should not become so attached to your work that you are afraid of a solid critique. We recommend that you share your essays with and seek feedback from one or two people—from a professional consultant or an individual who has insight into the application process—but that you limit your feedback loop thereafter. Because the application process is subjective, you will

*Long-Term Planning*

discover that as you add readers, you will also add new and different opinions. Soon, a multitude of alternatives might appear, and while these ideas will not necessarily be "right" or "wrong," as there are countless ways to market a single candidate's stories, they can create unnecessary uncertainty. We are not suggesting that you ignore critical feedback, but rather that you not create undue doubt. If one or two readers support your ideas and agree that your application needs minimal work, you are probably best off ending your feedback loop there and continuing the application process with confidence.

# October

## Complete and Submit First-Round Applications

As you approach the first-round application deadlines, which typically fall within the first two weeks of October, you should of course do whatever you can to submit your best work—but you should also focus on letting go once your application has been submitted. If you later realize that some part of your application included a typo, this is unfortunate, but it is not a reason to panic. Admissions committees are not looking for reasons to reject you; they are seeking to get to know you through your files. So, press submit, and start to look forward instead of back. At this time, you might consider a brief break of about one week to clear your head and recharge for the second round of applications. The application process can be exhausting, and you will need to be at your best to compete.

## Visit Remaining Target Schools

As we noted earlier, first-hand experience is crucial in that in it enables you to get to know a target MBA program better and also to more easily make a case for your fit with the school. Most class visit programs commence in October, just prior to first-round deadlines. If you plan to visit any additional schools, you should ideally do so before the first-round submission date, so that you can learn from your experience and apply your learning to your applications.

# November

## Prepare Second-Round Essays/Applications

With the first round behind you, you do not have much time to relax, given that second-round application deadlines are only nine or ten weeks away (early January). Get started on the applications for your next few target schools, recognizing that the second round is a de facto final round for most applicants. Generally, most candidates are admitted in the first two rounds and only truly unique/powerhouse candidates manage to eke their way into programs in Round 3.

## Plan Interviews with Target Schools

Good news—the admissions committee has read your first-round applications and… you have been invited to interview! Some interviews occur on campus with students or admissions staff. Other interviews take place with alumni in your city. Candidates will always fret about whether one kind of interview is better than the other, and admissions committees consistently tell applicants that all interviews are treated equally. The interviewer is not as important as you, the interviewee. To prepare for your interview, you should review your essays, and your resume in particular, and contemplate judgments and decisions that you have made. In 99% of cases, your interviewer will ask you questions only about your life (never inquiring about the economy, politics, etc.). Although the interview process can seem stressful, you should know the answers to all questions, because they are yours already.

# December

## Complete First-Round Interviews

First-round interviews will continue through December. You may wonder why a friend of yours was asked to interview in November and you were given a later interview decision. Stop worrying—the top schools do not show preference for candidates by inviting some ahead of others. The admissions committees read applications randomly and either ask individuals to interview as they complete the applications or will hold and then release interview invitations in batches. Either way, the timing is not important, but what is important is that you prepare thoroughly for the meeting and do your best. Again, review your own story and know it cold—your interviewer will inquire about *you*.

## Await First-Round Decisions

By December, first-round decisions will start to be announced. Some schools will release them all at once online, whereas others will slowly release them via phone calls or online over a period of a few weeks. As with interview invitations, if your friend hears from the school before you, you generally have no need to panic. Avoid the temptation to call the admissions office and ask whether a decision has been made about your candidacy. Admissions personnel are easily frustrated by such calls and will not give you the answers you seek. Sit back, try to be patient and the school will contact you in due time.

# January

## Submit Second-Round Applications

As you approach your second-round deadlines, which typically fall in the first two weeks of January, you should of course do whatever you can to submit your best work. As with any applications you submitted in the first round, though, you should also focus on letting go once your materials have been submitted. So, take a deep breath, submit your application and start looking forward instead of back.

## Await First-Round Decisions and Indecisions

If not by December, then by January (or early February at the very latest), your first-round decisions will be announced. Once again, avoid the temptation to call the admissions office and ask whether a decision has been made about your candidacy. Hopefully, you will be admitted at target schools across the board. Receiving a notification of "indecision," meaning that you have been placed on the school's waitlist, can be quite a frustrating turn of events. However, it is actually a positive sign—your target school does not want to lose the option to admit you.

When you are placed on the waitlist, you will likely get a letter from the admissions director at your target school. You should read this letter carefully and follow the school's instructions precisely. Some schools want no contact from you at all while you are waitlisted and will let you know of their decisions whenever they are made. Others will entertain additional letters from you and your recommenders, or will accept a new GMAT score or other new or supplementary materials. If you find yourself on a school's waitlist, the game is hardly over, and in some cases, the indecision may linger until the week before the MBA program is scheduled to begin. Some schools continue to admit students until the very last moment, so be prepared to exercise patience.

## Complete Second-Round Interviews

Second-round interview invitations should trickle out by the end of January, then a wave should be released in February and a few invitations will finally be released in March. As with first-round interviews, some second-round interviews occur on campus with students or admissions staff, while others take place with alumni in your city. Remember, as we stated earlier (see "November"), all interviews are treated equally. The interviewer is not as important as you, the interviewee. Although the interview process can seem stressful, you should know all the necessary answers.

Long-Term Planning

# Post-Application Stage

## Await Second-Round Decisions

Usually by March, second-round decisions will start to be announced and they will continue into April. Ideally, you have been diligent and have balanced ambition with realism as you applied. We hope that at this point, you will be popping the champagne and planning a vacation, getting ready for a summer/fall entry at a top business school.

## Apply for Scholarships/Student Loans (if applicable)

Most schools will award scholarships when they admit a candidate, and some will give you the chance to write yet another (!) essay—or two—to apply for their scholarships. Despite your fatigue at this point in the process, you should certainly hunker down one more time and write those scholarship essays. Business schools can be quite generous with financial aid. Applying for scholarships and student loans is pretty straightforward. Your letter of acceptance will likely include information on whom to contact in the school's finance aid office, and someone should shepherd you through the process.

## Start the Visa Process

If you are not an American, you will need to apply for a student visa, which may take some time. Fortunately, your future school will walk you through the process, which tends to be bureaucratic, but not necessarily difficult. As long as you are on top of your application and send it in with a few months to spare, you should have your visa in hand long before your first day at school.

# Brainstorming

Chapter 2

# *Brainstorming*

The goal of brainstorming is to reveal not just the experiences, but also—and more importantly—the stories that make you distinct from other business school applicants. Although conveying your responsibilities and the nature of your work, volunteer efforts and personal accomplishments is important, you will almost always be telling stories—each with a beginning, middle and end—to the admissions committee. To help you as you begin to contemplate your stories and uncover them one at a time, we have created a questionnaire, provided later in this chapter, which will serve as a guide.

## Professional Experiences

Professional experiences are judged not on the basis of the dollars involved, but on your actions. Whether you are telling the story of how you helped merge two multibillion-dollar firms or how you started a local bicycle shop, the admissions committee is more concerned with the intensity of your spirit than with monetary figures. Factual aspects provide context, but emotional aspects give your stories power. No matter how "small" an experience might seem, if you brought the entirety of your passion and creativity to it, it should make compelling reading for the admissions committee.

Although professional stories typically cover traditional business accomplishments (e.g., you closed the deal, found a new market niche), your "soft" achievements in the workplace should not be overlooked and can also be fodder for compelling essays. By "soft," we mean the more human, perhaps less quantifiable aspects of your work experiences, such as developing and implementing a mentorship program for interns, founding a workplace improvement committee or helping a struggling colleague. These stories can be just as powerful.

## Community/Volunteer Stories

Likewise, do not ignore your "hard" accomplishments from your community activities. You can prove your competencies and, more importantly, diversify your application and highlight your personal values by, for example, telling the story of how you ran a successful fundraiser for a local charity, coached a children's soccer team or helped an elderly neighbor with her taxes and financial planning. Although the scale of the accomplishment(s) may or may not be in proportion to your work achievements, scale is not what is relevant. The admissions committee is more concerned with your decision-making ability, actions and spirit.

## Personal Stories

Many applicants overlook their personal accomplishments when considering their candidacy for business school, but these stories have incredible potential to powerfully differentiate one candidate from another. You have sole ownership of your personal accomplishments—no one else can or will tell the same stories. To understand the nature of personal stories, consider these examples: a candidate who learned Spanish to read a book written by his great-grandfather or a candidate who helped house and educate a dislocated refugee—both have distinct and fascinating stories to tell. These might be extreme examples, but most candidates, at some point, have gone above and beyond in some way to help another or to push themselves. These stories are remarkably valuable and should definitely not be overlooked.

## The Process of Brainstorming

When you are brainstorming, "more is more" is definitely the rule. A compelling story is obviously the foundation of a profound essay, so the more exploration you do and the more stories you uncover—and can thus consider for inclusion in your application—the more likely you are to pinpoint the most effective options for your essays. We do not advise choosing a weak story and trying to make it compelling through the shrewd use of language. And do not confuse "weak story" with "unsuccessful result"—some candidates' most powerful essays are about times when they actually did *not* reach their goals or struggled significantly with something. Be exhaustive. Spend many hours brainstorming, and consider all the facets of your life. This upfront investment will pay dividends throughout your application process.

Also, as you brainstorm, try to consider each of your experiences from multiple angles. For example, the brand manager who brought a new product to market may think of this accomplishment as an example of leadership only, but the story can actually be used to illustrate several other aspects of the candidate's experiences. The brand manager may have conceived the idea (creativity) and pushed his/her firm to implement it (entrepreneurship), managed a staff and navigated internal conflicts (teamwork skills), dealt with sourcing issues or product attributes (revealing ethics), struggled along the path to success (failure/setbacks), etc. Do not accept your stories merely at face value, but take time to explore what they might represent in broader terms. (Please see the exercise at the end of this chapter for an example.)

Your brainstorming process is not necessarily exclusive to your own memory. Consider discussing your experiences with parents, supervisors, colleagues, friends, etc. (where appropriate), to generate additional stories and even discover how others view(ed) you and your accomplishments. Simply put, sometimes you will not understand where you have shined, and others may see a quality or skill you were not aware you possessed. These added perspectives will help create a fuller, richer picture for you to work with going forward.

Although there is no "right" page length for your brainstorming document, most candidates tend to exhaust themselves somewhere between 10 and 15 pages.

Brainstorming

# Brainstorming Questionnaire

**1.** List your major accomplishments/achievements (not responsibilities!) in each of your professional positions (see the example that follows). To the best of your ability, briefly describe the beginning, middle and end of what would constitute a story about these accomplishments.

EXAMPLE:

Company/Dates of Employment: *Recruiting Associates Inc.; Sept. 2004–Present*

Company Description (if company is not well known, be brief!): *ABC is a 300-person human resources consulting firm, operating out of Kansas City, Kansas.*

Department: *Corporate Recruiting*

Job Title: *Senior Consultant*

Accomplishment 1: *Established new accounting recruitment department*

- Beginning: *Approached management with idea to enter accounting recruitment market; persuaded management to dedicate human resources and $120K budget*

- Middle: *Managed staff of three; identified 80 credible candidates; held unique marketing events/career fairs to showcase candidates; aggressively built relationships with 60 manufacturers in tristate area*

- End: *Placed 37 candidates in first year; revenue of $420K; promoted; budget increased and additional human resources allocated*

Accomplishment 2: ...

- Beginning: ...

- Middle: ...

- End: ...

**2.** List your major accomplishments in each of your community activities, following a similar format (template below).

EXAMPLE:

Organization/Dates of Involvement: *Urban Kitchen; July 2005–Present*

Description of Organization: *Urban Kitchen aggregates unserved restaurant meals and serves this food to the less fortunate*

Role: *Shift Coordinator*

Hours Per Month: *16*

Accomplishment 1: *Raised funds for full-time general manager*

- Beginning: *Saw organization being stretched; identified need for general manager to recruit volunteers and oversee distribution*

- Middle: *Networked with existing corporate sponsors; identified available government grants; applied for grants from charitable foundations*

- End: *Received $55K in funding; full-time manager in place; 12 new volunteers are serving 15% more meals per week*

**3.** List your major accomplishments in each of your collegiate extracurricular activities, following the format shown in the examples for Questions 1 and 2.

*Brainstorming*

**4.** List any instances in which you have made a significant difference in another human being's life (i.e., helping solve a family problem, teaching a child to read, mentoring a coworker who is having trouble, etc.).

**5.** List the five personal accomplishments of which you are most proud (as they relate to yourself, not others—i.e., completed a marathon, published a poem in literary journal, overcame a fear of heights, traveled to 17 different countries, etc.).

**6.** List your academic accomplishments: awards, honors, distinctions, publications, etc. Briefly explain the nature of and selection criteria for each.

**7.** List any professional/community recognition that has been bestowed upon you.

**8.** Describe any conflicts you have had in professional or organizational settings and how you handled them.

**9.** Discuss any professional or personal setbacks or failures that you have experienced (not addressed in Question 8). Have you ever missed any opportunities, not achieved a goal or disappointed another person?

**10.** List your primary hobbies and interests, past and present.

**11.** List five words or phrases your friends/family would use to describe you. List five words or phrases you would use to describe yourself.

**12.** List all the countries to which you have traveled and your reason for doing so (i.e., business or pleasure).

**13.** List any language(s) your speak aside from your native tongue and your level of fluency in each.

**14.** Briefly, what are your short-term and long-term goals after business school?

**15.** List the reasons you feel you want/need to get an MBA. How do you believe an MBA program will prepare you to reach your goals, and why do you believe now is the best time to get this degree?

**16.** What do you want to learn in an MBA program? What will be your area of focus?

Brainstorming

# Essay Writing

## Chapter 3

# *Part I: Preparing Outlines for Your Essays*

Years of experience have proven to us at mbaMission that virtually every candidate is better off creating outlines for his/her essays before writing the first full drafts. You are a busy person—you are balancing work, studying for and taking the GMAT, engaging in community activities, trying to maintain a personal life and more. Why not bring some efficiency and organization to the essay writing process?

Truth be told, some candidates' first reaction to the concept of creating an outline rather than simply diving into writing the first draft is not a positive one. They imagine that this "extra" step will add time and complication to their application process when in fact, creating an outline can not only help streamline one's essay writing but also go a long way in boosting the resulting essays' effectiveness. By first taking the time to organize your thoughts in the form of shorter phrases and terms, you will more easily see how your story unfolds and ensure that no gaps occur in the information you are trying to convey. This means a stronger, more persuasive final essay and, in most cases, fewer rounds of editing and revision.

## The Outline as Roadmap

Think of your outline as a kind of roadmap, one that guides you smoothly from the beginning of your story to the end, noting each important milestone along the way. Each major heading—or, if you prefer, each bullet point—should therefore consist of a very brief summary of a bigger idea. In other words, it should capture your key point but should not include the background, explanation or descriptive details, leaving those for the first draft of the essay. Simply put, the key in creating your outline is to provide a concise overview of what you intend to write in your actual essay.

Essay Writing

When you are constructing your outline, you can use very informal language, and you do not need to worry about using full sentences or proper grammar. After all, you are not submitting your outline to anyone—it is for "internal use only," so to speak. Always remember that an outline should be just a brief overview of your longer essay. In general, we recommend that your outline be no longer than approximately 50% of the total word count allowed in the essay. Outlining a 500-word essay with eight bullet points of 100 words each is pointless—your outline will be longer than your final essay will be, and this will not facilitate a more organized, efficient or enjoyable writing experience.

## The Super Summary

Your first step in outlining any essay is to compose one very clear sentence that captures the key idea that ties your entire essay together. This "super summary" of your essay will enable you to focus your thoughts and structure your work, much like a thesis sentence would for a more scientific or theoretical text. This is a nuanced but important point (one that we explore in depth in Part II of this chapter): for your business school application essays, you are not attempting to use a thesis to "prove" a point factually but are trying to construct a narrative that describes a central idea or experience from your life. So, you may start out with a well-structured outline and a clear thesis, but these will likely be softened and made less explicit in your first and final drafts.

In Sample Essay A, which appears in full later in this section, the candidate is answering the question—"Describe an impact you have had on an individual, group or organization. How has this experience been valuable to you or others? (500 words)." As you will see, the applicant has chosen to write about his experience as a volunteer children's soccer coach. A good super summary for him to build his essay around might then be: *"Through creative motivational techniques and enthusiastic leadership, I helped maintain the spirits of a group of 12-year-old boys during a soccer season in which they lost almost all their games."*

This super summary works well because it presents the structure of the entire essay in one concise sentence. You now know exactly what the essay is going to discuss (the writer's challenging experience as a children's soccer coach one season) and how the essay will be focused. From this sentence, the candidate could then organize a structure for the essay, creating a loose outline of its key paragraphs, as follows:

Super Summary: *"Through creative motivational techniques and enthusiastic leadership, I helped maintain the spirits of a group of 12-year-old boys during a soccer season in which they lost almost all their games."*

Paragraph 1: Introduction to the challenges encountered with the team

Paragraph 2: Actions taken to resolve these challenges

Paragraph 3: Results of the actions taken

Paragraph 4: Lessons learned ("Takeaways")

# Breaking It Down

Now, to create a logical and defined structure for these paragraphs, some short bullet points can be added to support the central idea within each paragraph. Once this has been done, writing the actual essay becomes much less difficult. Consider the following:

Paragraph 1: Introduction to the challenges encountered with the team

- I inherited a kids' soccer team that had lost all its games in the previous season; knew I was facing an uphill battle

- Noticed low morale immediately; after we lost the first five games of the season, things got worse

- Saw parents yelling at each other and at referees

- Recognized that situation needed to change

Paragraph 2: Actions taken to resolve these challenges

- Negative Actions: Held parent meeting to propose positive attitudes; took difficult step and asked one abusive parent to leave the next game

- Positive Actions: No team wins, so I rewarded small victories on team; gave each player a nickname so that soccer was a special activity for them; gave post-game and post-practice award to "hardest working player"

Paragraph 3: Results of the actions taken

- Negative parents stayed away; kids felt less pressure

- Players started showing up for practice on time, listened more, more energetic on and off the field, began to have real fun and learn

- Won four of our six final games that season

- Was asked to coach the following year

Paragraph 4: Lessons learned ("Takeaways")

- Usually very goal oriented, I became entirely process oriented; found rewards in my players' small victories

- Did not enjoy banishing parents, but was tough and decisive when needed

And here is the actual essay, with footnoted comments, following this outline.

# Sample Essay A

"Describe an impact you've had on an individual, group or organization. How has this experience been valuable to you or others?" (500 words)

*When Dr. Gibson, the parent of a child on the soccer team I had just agreed to coach, turned over his whistle to me and said, "Good luck with the kids, but more so with the parents," I finally understood the challenge before me.[1] A new season was starting, but my team of 12-year-olds would have difficulty forgetting the last, in which they had lost 26 of 28 games. Even worse, we lost our first five games, so players started showing up late, parents began criticizing one another's kids and one parent stormed the field to confront a referee. Stunned, I knew I needed to take decisive action to rein in the chaos and salvage the season.[2]*

*First, I held a parents meeting during which I outlined a zero-tolerance policy: "Only encouragement from the sidelines" and "Each player will arrive 15 minutes before game time to prepare or will not play." Admittedly, as a 24-year-old, I was uncomfortable enforcing rules with adults twice my age, but I knew I had to remain firm. At our next game, I demanded that a referee remove an abusive fan—one of my players' parents! I also refused to let a player who had arrived 20 minutes late play. After enforcing these rules, I did not have another such problem again.[3]*

*With the parents "tamed," I began working on the players. I had to find new ways to make soccer fun. I started giving my players nicknames.*

Essay Writing

---

1   While the writer is following the structure of the outline, he is also clearly adding color to it, from the very first word. Thus, the outline serves its purpose as a structural foundation and not a mini essay.

2   The narrative structure belies the need for a definitive and "scientific" thesis statement. At the end of the broader introduction, the reader clearly understands the direction that the essay will take, but some mystery remains as to how the story will unfold.

3   Again, following the format of the outline, the writer uses the ideas that he has already developed and now brings in the details to create the essay's personality.

*Soon, our team consisted of "Sparky," "Lefty," "Red" and others—names that brought smiles to the kids' faces, even when we were losing. Then, I decided that after each practice and game, I would announce a "hardest working player" award. As expected, players competed aggressively for the title, as each was motivated to earn the recognition. Throughout the next few games, I ensured that different players got the award, which created a sense of pride and positive spirit.[1]*

*With this new attitude and dedication, and negativity a thing of the past, I managed to run more drills and plan strategies in practice— which now began on time. Soon, my team was passing the ball more, and players were staying in their positions. Suddenly, we won a game; everyone celebrated as though we had won the World Cup! Then, we won a few more—four of our final six! At the season's end, the parents asked that I coach the team again the next season. Of course, I accepted.[2]*

*From elementary school through college, I had always played soccer with true competitors and focused on winning. I was surprised I could take pride in watching two 12-year-olds pass the ball well, even if they ultimately lost it to a player on the other team. I felt a strong sense of ownership over those passes. No matter what I have experienced in my professional career, my greatest test has been remaining stern with my team's parents—I learned lessons in consistency and integrity that will remain with me throughout my life.[3]*

---

1 Note that as the writer progresses, he deviates a little bit from the outline—this is entirely acceptable! He breaks the positive and negative actions in two and develops them as separate paragraphs. This new structure actually works quite well, given that the positive and negative are independent ideas.

2 Again, in this paragraph, we see a reasonable deviation from the outline. Although most of the points in the outline are represented through the story, some points are not. For example, that the negative parents stayed away is not explicitly stated here, because this point has already been made in the previous paragraph.

3 A philosophical conclusion can be challenging to outline. The conclusion is derived from the story that develops; thus, the conclusion and the story as a whole may need to be considered in tandem. Here, the basic bullet points in the outline are again expanded upon, and, in fact, the final bullet is not even explored. Still the outline served well as a foundation for the essay, and the writer simply adapted and developed his more thoughtful conclusion here.

An outline should serve as a simple guide for writing a narrative, not dictate the essay's definitive and inalterable structure. If, while composing Sample Essay A, the writer had thought of a new takeaway or felt that the essay was taking shape in a slightly different way, that would be fine—the writer would simply need to revise the outline accordingly, ensuring that the revised outline still worked as a roadmap, effectively guiding the reader from the beginning of the story to the end, and that all the key milestones along the way made sense within context. The overarching idea here is to use the outline to get organized and to start in the right direction with a clear foundation.

## Outlines for Unconventional Essay Formats

Schools are beginning to introduce unconventional essay questions that ask candidates to provide content in ways other than the traditional written essay, such as audio files, videos and illustrations. Creating outlines for "essays" presented in these new formats is as important as it is for traditional essays—if not more—and this step should not be skipped. Candidates should consider the content they want to convey before devising the design they wish to use to present it. Fully understanding and crafting your content first via an outline will start you on the right track.

*Additional Sample Outline*

"Columbia Business School Essay 1/Personal Statement: What are your short-term and long-term post-MBA goals? How will Columbia Business School help you achieve these goals? (Recommended 750-word limit; 2009–2010 essay question)"

Super Summary: *My short-term goal of turning around a small manufacturer and long-term goal of starting my own private equity fund will be directly facilitated by a Columbia Business School MBA.*

Essay Writing

1. Goal Section

    A. Intro/Context

        • Honed expertise in operations with world leader in pharmaceutical manufacturing

    B. Short-Term Goals

        • Will purchase a small, inefficient manufacturer in an "old economy" industry and lead a turnaround

    C. Long-Term Goals

        • Leverage credibility via successful turnaround and begin to develop a portfolio of stable, old-economy manufacturing firms; possibly even help revitalize industries on verge of "extinction"

2. Why Columbia Section

    A. General Management (broad lead-in)

        • I am focused in operations and need the core curriculum to bolster my existing skills

    B. Entrepreneurship

        • Naturally want to pursue this area with my plans

        • Entrepreneurial sounding board

        • Entrepreneurial Greenhouse

        • The Lang Center and Fund

&bull; Courses: "Entrepreneurial Finance" with Morten Sorenson; "Launching New Ventures" with Professor Clifford Schorer

## C. Finance

&bull; Future plans combine existing background, entrepreneurship and finance

&bull; Clear emphasis on finance at Columbia via such a large faculty—learn from many minds

&bull; Coursework: "Legends in Value Investing" with Professor Bruce Greenwald (phenomenal guest lectures); "Earnings Quality and Fundamental Analysis" with Professor Doron Nissim

## D. Environmental Factors

&bull; Campus visit: Warm interactions with professors (professor followed up with me via email); great interaction with students (went for beers after class); very positive impression

&bull; New York: Unparalleled location for private equity and entrepreneurship

## 3. Conclusion

# *Part II: Writing Effective Essays*

For some applicants, writing business school essays may be an entirely new writing experience. While some may have written history essays or English literature papers in college, for example, others may not have written any essays at all. But, in most cases, those who do have some experience writing formal essays were asked to prove an argument in their text, not communicate an image through an introspective personal essay.

In high school and college, most students are taught to write using something called the *hourglass model.* Following this model, the writer starts with a broad introduction of the topic to be discussed, narrows his/her scope to a particular thesis, proves or supports this thesis with evidence and then presents broad conclusions based on the evidence.

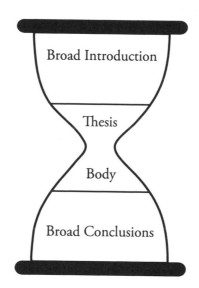

This traditional and formal way of writing can be quite effective when one is introducing a concrete argument, as shown in the following example:

*Because Bill Murray first established himself as a star through* Saturday Night Live, Caddyshack *and* Ghostbusters, *most still regard him as a "pure" comedian. In recent years, however, Murray has taken on far more serious roles, though most still included elements of comedy, such as his portrayal of a dispirited industrialist in* Rushmore *and a depressed movie star in* Lost in Translation. *Ironically, in his more serious films, Murray espouses a confused sense of morality—toying with adultery in both, for example—but in his "pure" comedies, he represents a clear and simple passion for what are widely regarded as traditional American values—patriotism/anti-communism in* Stripes, *for example, and heroism/entrepreneurialism in* Ghostbusters. *A close study of the Murray comedic-canon reveals him to be a kind of jester, defending America from threats and rallying others to uphold the principles outlined in the U.S. Constitution.*

Whether you agree with the statements made about Murray in this sample is entirely beside the point. We present this just as an illustration of formal writing, which involves a broad opening that then narrows to a very clear thesis. In contrast, for a business school candidate to write this way in an essay about him/herself would be somewhat absurd. If, for example, a school were to ask, "What makes you distinct as an applicant?" you would be ill advised to write the following in response:

*Ice hockey is a national passion and way of life in Canada. As a Canadian myself, I have been playing hockey constantly since I was three years old, when I laced up my skates for the first time. Each year throughout my youth, my father would build an ice rink in our backyard, where I would spend countless hours playing and practicing hockey. I have now played, coached and even refereed ice hockey for two decades. Further, I am an avid follower of the National Hockey League and international competitions, frequently traveling to games around the world. Clearly, my passion for ice hockey distinguishes me from other candidates and is indicative of a broader energy and passion that will enable me to stand out as an MBA student at your school.*

Essay Writing

Although this example is written "tongue in cheek" for illustrative purposes, we hope it shows just how dry some writing can be. When you are writing an essay for any purpose, you need to keep your target audience in mind, but when you are drafting an application essay in particular, you must take care to be sensitive to that audience's special circumstances. Admissions readers see literally thousands of essays each year, reading similar compositions all day, every day, for months at a time. How can you connect with such an audience? To effectively do so, your first step is to forget your preconceived notions about essay writing and to concentrate on composing personalized *narratives*.

# Consider a Narrative Approach

Narratives are categorized by a more subtle approach to writing, wherein the central facts are not just bluntly introduced but are presented in a way that lets them speak for themselves and paint a rounded picture of an experience. Further, in the case of your business school applications, for which the narratives need to be about you, the candidate, the text needs to be written from the first-person perspective—using "I," "me" and "my," rather than "one," "he" and "his."

Let us return to the example of writing about hockey as a way to reveal your passions. Consider the following sentences:

Example A: *"Ice hockey is a national passion and way of life in Canada. As a Canadian myself, I have been playing hockey constantly since I was three years old, when I laced up my skates for the first time. Each year throughout my youth, my father would build an ice rink in our back yard, where I would spend countless hours playing and practicing hockey."*

Example B: *"When I turned three, my grandmother bought me my first pair of ice skates, which I refused to take off—even when I went to bed at night—for the*

Essay Writing

*next full week. After two years of what my father now refers to as 'constant beg-ging,' I managed to convince him to build a full-size ice rink in our backyard."*

Which of these sample introductions resonates with you and creates a more compelling image of the person you are reading about? We expect that it is the latter! The first follows more of a traditional essay approach, and the second takes a narrative approach. So, what are some of the key differences between these two options?

A narrative is characterized by the **first-person perspective**. Consider the line "ice hockey is a national passion and a way of life in Canada" from Example A. This is a statement of fact that focuses on things other than the writer, not a first-person description of a personal experience like we see in Example B: "When I turned three, my grandmother bought me my first pair of ice skates, which I refused to take off—even when I went to bed at night—for the next full week." Complementing this first-person perspective is a sense of **ownership**. "Ice hockey is a national passion and a way of life" is not a statement that applies exclusively to the writer. In fact, this objective statement could be made by just about anyone (and statements that are not specific to the writer are especially to be avoided in application essay writing). In contrast, it is improbable that many people would share the exact same experience of having had their grandmother buy them skates when they were three and then wearing them nonstop for an entire week—which means the chances of two people both writing the sentence "When I turned three, my grandmother bought me my first pair of ice skates, which I refused to take off—even when I went to bed at night—for the next full week" are almost nil. By creating truly personal sentences based on your particular experience, you alone <u>own</u> the story, and this can help set you apart from the competition when you are applying to business school.

One concern of many applicants is that this approach might be difficult to execute, but we firmly believe that it is actually easier than traditional essay writing because it allows the writer to simply consider and convey actual events and experiences as they occurred. Writing a narrative does not require using long, complex sentences or sophisticated adjectives with multiple syllables. In fact, **simplicity** is truly the rule. Once again, consider Example B. The language is not particularly elaborate—"convince" may be the most complex word in the two sentences! Furthermore, when writing a simple narrative (they can be more complicated if you have the skill, but they do not need to be to make your point), you can ease your execution by maintaining the momentum in your story—ensuring that your description of the experience is constantly moving forward. To do this, you can continuously ask yourself, "And then what happened?" and generally, you should be able to keep reporting the events as they occurred. As long as your core story is strong and you maintain a connection from sentence to sentence, writing the details of your narrative should enable you to create an interesting essay. After all, you are simply relating a personal experience you had, not trying to prove a thesis or make disconnected facts fit. On the other hand, when you have started your essay with "Ice hockey is a national passion and way of life in Canada," knowing how to answer the question "And then what happened?" and getting the story to unfold from there is much more difficult.

In addition, writing an essay using a narrative approach facilitates a certain **earnestness**. In Example A, the writer states, "As a Canadian myself, I have been playing hockey constantly since I was three years old..." While this is not as pushy as telling the reader straight out "I am a great hockey player," it still uses stark language and a rather boastful tone. In Example B, however, the reader learns that the individual is passionate about ice hockey, but he does so by *witnessing* the writer's passion rather than simply being told it exists. The reader naturally understands it.

## Showing Versus Telling

Indeed, a journalistic maxim is at play here—"Show, don't tell!"—which captures the essence of narrative writing. Instead of "telling" your reader that you are passionate about ice hockey, for example, show the reader by relating a personal experience. Consider the following examples of telling versus show-ing:

Example C:

*Tell*: *My aunt loves all animals and will do anything to help one or save one. Sometimes she goes to extreme lengths to help a dog or a cat. She will spend weeks or even months trying to locate an owner.*

*Show*: *When my aunt found a stray cat, she housed it for three weeks and started a poster campaign to locate the owner. Three weeks later, she got a desperate phone call, thanking her for her persistence.*

Example D:

*Tell*: *I love to travel and have visited more than 20 countries on four continents, primarily in Latin America, where I became fluent in Spanish and Portuguese.*

*Show*: *Peru, Ecuador, Columbia, Brazil and Argentina—after six months in these countries, I found myself speaking rapid, colloquial Spanish and Portuguese with locals.*

Again, you will notice that while the underlying messages are the same, the methods for conveying the message are different. When you *show* an idea or experience in your writing, you invite the reader into your story and have a better chance of maintaining his/her attention from that point on. However, business school applicants, who must conform to set word limits for the essays they submit, commonly worry that showing rather than telling will require more words—but this is not necessarily true. If you reread Examples C and D, you will see that a great deal can be accomplished and conveyed in the same number of words or less. Moreover, in both examples, the "show" versions actually use fewer words than their corresponding "tell" versions.

Essay Writing

For years, Harvard Business School has asked candidates the following question: "What are your three most substantial accomplishments and why do you view them as such? (600-word limit)." Even with only approximately 200 words for each of the three accomplishments to be covered in this 600-word essay, the writer can still develop a complete story, as shown in the following example:

> *I joined the board of the BlackJack Theatre Company three weeks after a failed audit and the surprise resignation of the executive director (ED). At my first meeting, I persuaded the board to divide up the names of our 400 subscribers and call each to discuss our commitment to change. I was stunned to learn that only 12 chose not to renew and that 30 actually donated to the "save the theatre" campaign I had initiated. Building on this momentum, I approached area restaurants, which benefit from our 64 nights of use each year, for donations and applied for a government "nonprofit stabilization grant," quickly raising $34,350—enough to retire much of our debt. After eight hours of debate about a new ED, I prevailed in championing Michael, an entrepreneurially minded playwright who emphasized the balance between art and finance. In his first season, Michael assembled a conservative, crowd-pleasing schedule, and we broke even. Soon, the board asked me to assume the role of president—I accepted. I had had no previous experience in the nonprofit world and take great pride in having helped save the BlackJack, a 20-year-old civic institution. The worst is now behind us. The main drama at the BlackJack is back on the stage, where it belongs.*

Let's go through a quick checklist to see what this essay accomplished:

✓ **First-person perspective**: Indeed, this is a very specific experience that is told in the first person, using "I," "my" and "me."

✓ **Ownership**: This essay is "owned" by the writer—it is not at all generic. Although someone else may have helped turn around a struggling theatre at some point, the specific details of the story create a personal connection that make the piece undeniably that of the writer.

✓ **Simplicity**: The language is very simple—no five-syllable words are used. The sentence structure is basic and clear.

✓ **Earnestness**: The writer does not brag to get his point across. He did not directly state, "I am an entrepreneurially and socially minded individual and proved this when I led the turnaround of a nonprofit," nor did he need to. This very point is ultimately made, but the reader's attention is held by the power of the story itself.

✓ **Show, don't tell**: The writer simply presents the events as they occurred and lets the story do the work. He does not tell the reader how to feel, but instead allows the story to make the impression.

Essay Writing

One additional concept that is crucial to effective writing is **connectivity**—the "and then what happened?" factor. In an effective narrative essay, each sentence serves as a crucial link in the story. Remove a sentence from this sample essay, read the piece again and see if is still makes sense. We do this in the following example, and the story simply does not work:

*I joined the board of the BlackJack Theatre Company three weeks after a failed audit and the surprise resignation of the executive director (ED). I was stunned to learn that only 12 chose not to renew and that 30 actually donated to the "save the theatre" campaign I had initiated.*

"Who is renewing what?" the reader might ask. Clearly, information that is important to the narrative is missing.

In the following example, we again remove a sentence, and again the story ceases to make sense.

*Building on this momentum, I approached area restaurants, which benefit from our 64 nights of use each year, for donations and applied for a government "nonprofit stabilization grant," quickly raising $34,350—enough to retire much of our debt. In his first season, Michael assembled a conservative, crowd-pleasing schedule, and we broke even. Soon, the board asked me to assume the role of president—I accepted.*

In this case, the reader would be left wondering "Who is Michael?" or "What happened during the season?" Removing even one sentence means that crucial information is missing, proving that this is a "tight" narrative.

Read the following essay and look for the same elements:

Please describe a time when you coached, trained, or mentored a person or group. (500 words or less)

*At Snacks International (SI), the title Summer Intern was a license to get coffee. How did I know? I had interned with the company and actually counted the number of cups—126—I was asked to fetch while there. When I later joined SI full-time, I asked my supervisor if I could oversee the summer intern program, and he was "delighted to pass it off." Thus, I unceremoniously became Intern Coordinator.*

*I then met with SI's Brand Managers and asked each to complete a simple questionnaire on summer hiring needs. I quickly identified a rather obvious trend—while our seasonal ice cream and sports drink departments could outline multiple summer projects, our hot tea, coffee and prepared soup departments could not define any. So, rather than simply distributing our five summer interns evenly across the five departments that year, I placed them where they were actually needed. After all, training interns is difficult when they have no work to do.*

*In advance of our interns' arrival, I prepared folders with org charts, employee conduct policies, coupons for leisure activities and descriptions* of major summer projects for our arriving interns. Then, I met with each individually about their projects, which included researching alternative packaging options and analyzing our advertising spend on certain drinks, to establish deadlines and deliverables.

I let the interns know my door was always open and casually checked in with them at our daily firm-wide meeting. On Friday afternoons, each had a standing appointment with me, and every second Friday, their Brand Managers joined us for a project update. I had to laugh aloud during my first meeting with Shirley when she remarked that she was doing "real work" while a friend was "just getting coffee for a bond trader."

After four weeks, all our interns were on track with their projects—or so I thought. One afternoon, Christine came to me and said she was unsure of her analysis of our wholesaling alternatives and terrified of presenting her project to our VPs. I discovered that she had limited data available and used my relationships to help her source information from wholesalers. I felt with the right numbers in her hands, Christine could handle the analysis. I volunteered to meet with her to focus her study, and her project came together quickly. However, her fear of public speaking was the bigger challenge. I told her if she wanted to "practice, practice, practice," I would be available—always. I listened to Christine present daily during her final two weeks, and we had four practice sessions her final weekend. After her presentation, Christine literally leapt in the air and said she had "nailed it," which was true: her manager cited her presentation when Christine received her full-time offer.

Christine was not the only one given an offer—all the interns were asked to return, and four accepted. Today, we have eight interns annually, five summer and three winter. Each season, our program grows more robust, and it has become our sole source for recruiting junior staff.

Essay Writing

✓ **First-person perspective**: Again, this is a very specific experience that is told in the first person, using "I," "my" and "me."

✓ **Ownership**: Details like the 126 coffee deliveries clearly link the essay specifically to this writer. This is not "anyone's" story.

✓ **Simplicity**: The language is very simple: "unceremoniously" is the most sophisticated word used. The sentence structure is basic and clear.

✓ **Earnestness**: The writer does not simply declare "I was an effective manager" or "I ran an excellent internship program." His actions and results, as presented as part of the unfolding story, speak for themselves—the revamped intern program and the interns involved are shown to have succeeded, thereby illustrating the writer's effectiveness.

✓ **Show, don't tell**: The writer lets the story do the work and make an impression; he does not tell the reader how to feel or what to think.

✓ **Connectivity**: If a sentence were removed, the flow of the essay would be disrupted and the story would become confused.

# Conflict Is Good

Let us return to some elements from the beginning of this chapter as we contemplate the structure of the essay. It is important to keep in mind that every story must involve a clear conflict. By this, we mean conflict in the literary sense, not in the physical or emotional sense (no one wants to hear about you hotheadedly instigating repeated confrontations). In literary terms, conflict occurs when an oppositional force helps shape the story. So, a story that presents you, the hero of the story, enjoying a very smooth ride toward victory will not be as interesting or exciting as a story in which you suffered some bumps and bruises along the way.

For example, most people would find the story of a rookie runner beating an experienced marathoner at the finish line significantly more compelling than the story of an experienced marathoner beating all his fellow runners by a wide margin, never experiencing any competition. The former scenario involves a conflict in the form of an unexpected upset, whereas the latter presents a situation with no inherent surprise or suspense. So, as you work to identify stories to showcase in your application essays, consider the hurdles you have overcome in your life, because those narratives are the ones that will allow you to shine more brightly.

With this new perspective in mind, we will now revisit the essays we have already introduced thus far in this chapter.

In the brief piece about the BlackJack Theatre Company, the central conflict is introduced immediately: the theatre is teetering as the result of a scandal, and the writer/hero is trying to be resourceful in saving the day.

In the longer piece about the Snacks International internship program, the central conflict is revealed later in the essay. The writer/hero is initially quite successful in smoothly taking control of the program and giving it the necessary structure to succeed, but then, the intern Christine appears in his office in desperate need of help. This is not what he had planned! Still, the writer/hero responds to the challenge and proves his value to Christine—and thus to the reader.

In Part I of this chapter, we include an essay about a youth soccer coach who is immediately challenged by the players and their parents and is forced to respond. If he had not stepped up to this challenge and instead had allowed himself to be bullied, he would have no story to tell. The writer/hero's personal reaction to the situation and the change he brings about—in his players, their parents and himself—in response to it are what shape the story and make it interesting.

So, every story should involve a clear conflict—an oppositional force of some kind—to hold the reader's attention and maintain the narrative's momentum. In addition, well-written narratives, even those of 500 words or less, should have the following structural elements:

- **Introduction/Exposition**: The introduction provides the context for the story, enabling the reader to understand the characters and the setting in which the conflict exists.

- **Rising action**: During the rising action, the writer introduces obstacles to the resolution of the central conflict that test the story's hero as he/she strives to reach his/her goal.

- **Climax**: The climax is a moment of change, a turning point that determines whether the hero will ultimately succeed or fail.

- **Falling action**: During the falling action, the action winds down and the story approaches its close.

- **Conclusion/Dénouement**: During the conclusion, the story is brought to a close with the hero's ambitions either satisfied or unsatisfied. Sometimes the author may also reflect briefly on the outcome.

To illustrate, let us identify the structural elements as they appear in the essay about the youth soccer coach:

"Describe an impact you've had on an individual, group or organization. How has this experience been valuable to you or others?" (500 words)

*When Dr. Gibson, the parent of a child on the soccer team I had just agreed to coach, turned over his whistle to me and said, "Good luck with the kids, but more so with the parents," I finally understood the challenge before me. A new season was starting, but my team of 12-year-olds would have difficulty forgetting the last, in which they had lost 26 of 28 games. Even worse, we lost our first five games, so players started showing up late, parents began criticizing one another's kids and one parent stormed the field to confront a referee. Stunned, I knew I needed to take decisive action to rein in the chaos and salvage the season.[1]*

*First, I held a parents meeting during which I outlined a zero-tolerance policy: "Only encouragement from the sidelines" and "Each player will arrive 15 minutes before game time to prepare or will not play." Admittedly, as a 24-year-old, I was uncomfortable enforcing rules with adults twice my age, but I knew I had to remain firm.[2] At our next game, I demanded that a referee remove an abusive fan—one of my players' parents! I also refused to let a player who had arrived 20 minutes late play. After enforcing these rules, I did not have another such problem again.[3]*

*With the parents "tamed," I began working on the players. I had to find new ways to make soccer fun. I started giving my players nicknames. Soon, our team consisted of "Sparky," "Lefty," "Red" and others—names that brought smiles to the kids' faces, even when we were losing. Then, I decided that after each practice and game, I would announce a "hardest working player" award. As expected, players competed aggressively for the title, as each was motivated to earn the recognition. Throughout the next few games, I ensured that different players got the award, which created a sense of pride and positive spirit.*

*With this new attitude and dedication, and negativity a thing of the past, I managed to run more drills and plan strategies in practice—*

Essay Writing

---

1  Sometimes a single sentence can provide an introduction, though in this case, the conflict (between the coach and the team/parents) is gradually introduced throughout the entire first paragraph.

2  In the rising action (however brief in a 500-word essay), we see the obstacles the protagonist faces and his struggle to resolve them.

3  Here the climax occurs—the protagonist takes a dramatic stand and has a parent ejected! He also refuses to let a player who did not follow the rules take part in the game. He proves himself in doing so.

*which now began on time. Soon, my team was passing the ball more, and players were staying in their positions. Suddenly, we won a game; everyone celebrated as though we had won the World Cup! Then, we won a few more—four of our final six! At the season's end, the parents asked that I coach the team again the next season. Of course, I accepted.[1]*

*From elementary school through college, I had always played soccer with true competitors and focused on winning. I was surprised I could take pride in watching two 12-year-olds pass the ball well, even if they ultimately lost it to a player on the other team. I felt a strong sense of ownership over those passes. No matter what I have experienced in my professional career, my greatest test has been remaining stern with my team's parents—I learned lessons in consistency and integrity that will remain with me throughout my life.[2]*

The same elements can (and should) be included, even when the writer has limited word count with which to work. Even with a shorter essay, the five major stages of the story are clear:

*I joined the board of the BlackJack Theatre Company three weeks after a failed audit and the surprise resignation of the executive director (ED).[3] At my first meeting, I persuaded the board to divide up the names of our 400 subscribers and call each to discuss our commitment to change. I was stunned to learn that only 12 chose not to renew and that 30 actually donated to the "save the theatre" campaign I had initiated. Building on this momentum, I approached area restaurants, which benefit from our 64 nights of use each year, for donations and applied for a government "nonprofit stabilization grant," quickly raising $34,350—enough to retire much of our debt. After eight hours of debate about a new ED,*

---

1  In this portion of the story, the action "falls." The protagonist is no longer being tested but is working unabated toward his goals and seeing the results of his actions.

2  In this conclusion we see the protagonist's dreams realized. In addition, the writer/hero reflects on the experience, in response to the "How has this question been valuable to you or others" portion of the question.

3  **Introduction:** the stage is set and the conflict is clear. This theatre is in turmoil!

*I prevailed in championing Michael, an entrepreneurially minded play-wright who emphasized the balance between art and finance.[4] In his first season, Michael assembled a conservative, crowd-pleasing schedule, and we broke even. Soon, the board asked me to assume the role of president— I accepted.[5] I had had no previous experience in the nonprofit world and take great pride in having helped save the BlackJack, a 20-year-old civic institution. The worst is now behind us.[6] The main drama at the Black-Jack is back on the stage, where it belongs.[7]*

# A Special Focus on Introductions

If a writer is going to struggle, then he/she will likely do so at the very be-ginning of the writing process. Even with a strong outline in hand, crafting those first few words or phrases can often be challenging. In this section, we focus on composing introductions in hopes of helping you more easily overcome this hurdle when you begin drafting your business school essays.

## A Powerful Opening Line

*"Call me Ishmael."*

*"It was the best of times. It was the worst of times."*

*"It was a pleasure to burn."*

Some who read these lines may recognize them from the novels from which they came: Herman Melville's *Moby Dick*, Charles Dickens's *A Tale of Two Cities* and Ray Bradbury's *Fahrenheit 451*, respectively. However, fewer will have read these novels and some may be completely unfamiliar with these

---

4  **Rising action:** we witness the protagonist's ups and downs as he tries to "right the ship."
5  **Climax:** the protagonist is successful!
6  **Falling action:** because the essay is short, the falling action here is by necessity quite brief. We learn that the drama is over and the protagonist is pleased with the outcome of his efforts.
7  **Conclusion:** the institution has been saved and things have returned to normal.

novels and their authors—yet they may still recognize these opening lines. Our point? A powerful first line can stick with people long after they have finished reading a story, and sometimes even when they have not read the story at all!

# Maintaining the Mystery

While you do not need to write with the flair and drama of internationally acclaimed authors, you should carefully consider your opening statements and ensure that you are capturing your reader's imagination.

Consider three of the introductory sentences we have offered thus far in this chapter:

*I joined the board of the BlackJack Theatre Company three weeks after a failed audit and the surprise resignation of the executive director.*

*At Snacks International, the title Summer Intern was a license to get coffee.*

*When Dr. Gibson, the parent of a child on the soccer team I had just agreed to coach, turned over his whistle to me and said, "Good luck with the kids, but more so with the parents," I finally understood the challenge before me.*

These openers are designed to "tease" and naturally compel the reader to want to read on to unravel the mystery of the failing theatre, the joke of an internship program, the insanity of soccer parents. Many prospective MBAs give far too much away in the opening sentences of their application essays and present the solution to the story's central conflict right away (through a "tell"), which only succeeds in losing the reader immediately. (Remember, if you lose the reader, you risk losing your admissions offer, too.)

Consider the following examples, which present no mystery at all:

*I was very fortunate to have been an active board member as we saved the Black-Jack Theatre Company from a very serious scandal.*

*At Snacks International, I took over a long-ignored internship program and transformed it into a crucial employee pipeline.*

*When I coached soccer, I faced many unreasonable and overbearing parents and was forced to get tough with them, ultimately winning them over.*

Many MBA aspirants start their business school application essays with these types of openers. But where do you go from there? What can the reader really learn about you or the story you want to tell after one of these openings? Very little, unfortunately, and giving away the crux of your narrative in the first sentence makes writing the rest of the essay much more difficult. So, keep in mind that a narrative starts with a "blast" and then slowly unfolds—it should never solve the riddle in the first sentence.

# Historical Versus Anecdotal Opening

Many business school candidates choose to take a straightforward, historical approach to their stories in their essays. Nothing is fundamentally wrong with this tactic, and it can be an easy way to organize an essay. However, when a writer takes a historical approach, beginning the essay with straightforward chronological facts rather than something more compelling, he/she may ignore possibilities for a more focused and gripping introduction. For example, under certain circumstances, an anecdotal opening can better grab the reader's interest. Consider the following example of a historical opening:

*To the shock of my friends and family, I eschewed Wall Street and instead, of all things, opened a flower shop in midtown Manhattan. I was on the front lines, struggling to bring in new customers and traveling around the world in search of exotic products. In time, I learned to advertise selectively (on electronic billboards in local office buildings) and devel-*

*oped relationships with suppliers, particularly one in Peru, with whom I obtained an exclusive on a rare cousin of the Heliconia flower.*

This introduction is very direct and informative and entirely acceptable. However, the writer might be more successful in capturing the reader's attention if he/she instead uses an anecdotal opening, as shown in the following example:

*A crowd five deep assembled on the street to stare at the bright yellow Peruvian Heliconia in the window of my flower shop, the end result of three trips to the small South American country and two months of negotiations with the U.S. Department of Customs and Border Protection. Beaming, I opened my doors and said, "Come in"—and did they ever! Twenty customers immediately packed my store, and throughout the day, more and more continued to arrive, thanks to word of mouth. That day, the offer I had declined from Morgan Stanley nine months earlier completely vanished from my mind, and the flower shop has been my sole focus ever since.*

In the anecdotal version, much of the same basic information is conveyed, but the visual appeal is much stronger—the author paints a more colorful and complete picture. Again, one style of opening is not necessarily right and the other is not wrong. What matters is that you are comfortable with whichever one you choose. So take time to consider which one is a better fit with the narrative you intend to present. Depending on your story, an anecdotal opening may more easily allow you to capture the imagination of your reader. (In truth, however, this all comes down to execution—a strong writer could effectively execute either approach.)

## Leading with Your Best

Many candidates feel that they must start their essays by offering a time frame and a job position, but beginning your essay chronologically is not

*Essay Writing*

crucial. So, some might start a story by reaching back into their histories to create context. Let's take a look at such an example of an introduction for a question about a time when a candidate did something unexpected (in this case, shaking up a real estate portfolio).

> *I joined GPT Corp. in 2006, right out of college, knowing that I was entering a conservative culture. As a summer intern and then a member of the managerial rotational program, I was expected to listen and learn, taking on projects given to me by others. When I graduated from the rotational program and became a manager of GPT's $70M real estate portfolio, I could finally make my mark.*

This sample introduction offers a lot of backstory, but the most impressive part of the writer's story—managing a $70M real estate portfolio—is not mentioned until the third sentence, after the reader first learns about the candidate's less relevant or impressive work.

An alternative example follows, in which the writer leads with his best:

> *Before I felt I could legitimately call myself "manager" of GPT Corp.'s $70M real estate portfolio, I believed I needed to personally visit each of our 19 facilities, from Anchorage, Alaska, to Jacksonville, Florida.*

This introduction—which is only one sentence long, rather than three—not only introduces the reader to the individual's high-level position right away, but also initiates the story's action much earlier. This both captures the reader's attention more readily and leaves the writer with more words to use to tell the rest of the narrative.

# Non-Introduction Introduction

Indeed, the second example in the previous section is an illustration of "leading with your best" *as well as* what we call the "non-introduction introduction." Because candidates often feel they must follow the hourglass model of essay writing they first learned in high school, many end up crafting long and often uninteresting introductions that do not convey anything important. In the case of business school admissions essays, the writer is typically better served by simply launching into the action of his/her story and expecting that the reader will remain interested throughout the remainder of the narrative.

Once again, consider these three sample introductions:

*I joined the board of the BlackJack Theatre Company three weeks after a failed audit and the surprise resignation of the executive director.*

*At Snacks International, the title Summer Intern was a license to get coffee.*

*When Dr. Gibson, the parent of a child on the soccer team I had just agreed to coach, turned over his whistle to me and said, "Good luck with the kids, but more so with the parents," I finally understood the challenge before me.*

None of these examples includes a long "windup" to set the stage for the coming action. Instead, the writer introduces the story he/she wants to tell by beginning the narrative in the midst of the action. This approach, like leading with one's best (see previous section), both engages the reader in the story right away and minimizes word use, so more space is available to include more important details of the candidate's narrative.

## Overrepresenting Your Overrepresentation

Sometimes certain individuals in the MBA applicant pool—particularly male investment bankers and Indian software engineers—worry that they are overrepresented. As a result, they struggle with the idea of how to stand out in their essays from the hundreds, if not thousands, of other qualified candidates who may have similar work experience stories to tell. These applicants cannot change their past professional choices, of course, but they *can* change the way they introduce themselves to admissions committees. Consider the following examples:

*As an investment banker, I grew accustomed to the long hours, waiting for that final piece of data I needed to finish an important presentation.*

*Managing a team to code a new software product for ABC Corp., I meticulously checked my work and that of my teammates, knowing that any glitch could ruin us.*

In these examples, the candidate mistakenly—and rather blatantly—introduces the reader to the very overrepresentation about which he/she is concerned. Many applicants feel they must start their application essays by stating their title, company name or core responsibilities, but as we see here, doing so is unhelpful in making the candidate stand out or in capturing the reader's attention. More likely, such introductory sentences can immediately give the reader pause and make him/her think, "Here we go again."

So, overrepresented candidates need to consider their introductory lines quite carefully. Using an anecdotal introduction or leading with his/her best would both be preferable options, in such situations. These would allow the candidate to immediately immerse the reader in the action of a situation or present a special aspect of his/her position, as illustrated in the following examples:

*At 5:30 pm, I could rest easy. The deadline for all other offers had passed. At that point, I knew that shareholders had finally seen the value in our offer.* (Anecdotal opening)

*Managing a 12-person team, half in Silicon Valley and half in Pakistan, I felt I needed to first establish a unified culture.* (Leading with one's best)

In the anecdotal opening example, the banker candidate avoids a drab self-introduction and instead engages the reader in an unraveling mystery. In the example of leading with a standout aspect of one's job (leading with one's best), the software engineer candidate introduces him-/herself not as a "coder" but as a multinational manager. Every applicant—whether he/she is truly overrepresented in the MBA candidate pool or just fears so—can and should explore these alternative openings for his/her story to avoid the possible pitfalls of overrepresentation.

# Famous Quotations

Beginning an essay with a famous or eloquent quotation is a common practice and one that business school candidates can also use to capture a reader's attention. For example, an applicant might use a quotation as the very first line of their essay:

> *"The best executive is the one who has sense enough to pick good men to do what he wants done, and self-restraint enough to keep from meddling with them while they do it."*
>
> *— Theodore Roosevelt*

*Roosevelt's words are as true today as when he spoke them. The essence of a manager is…*

Another option is to embed the quotation within the first line of the essay, as follows:

*As Peter F. Drucker said, "Management is doing things right; leadership is doing the right things." I have found the distinction between management and leadership especially important…*

There is really only one rule about using quotations: do not overdo it! One grand quotation per application (not per essay!) is plenty and is certainly not mandatory. When deciding whether to include a quotation in an essay, consider the following:

- Does the quotation fit the essay's super summary?

- Does the quotation reflect who you are or what you believe?

- Does the quotation enhance the essay?

If the answers to these questions are all "yes," then making the quotation a part of your narrative might be a good idea.

# A Special Focus on Word Count

In general, sticking as closely to requested word limits as possible is a good idea. Doing so indicates to the admissions committee not only that you pay attention to and can follow directions (which reflects positively on you as a potential student who will be required to follow numerous guidelines throughout the course of the MBA program) but also that you are willing to put in the work required to convey your story effectively within the stated parameters. Also, you show respect for the school as well as for the admissions committee members, who must sort through thousands of essays each week. The rule of thumb is to not exceed the school's requested word count by more than 5%, though of course, the fewer extra words you include, the better—and minimizing any risk of a negative impression resulting from exceeding the set word count is best.

Some schools specify a maximum page count instead of a word count. In such cases, pay close attention to requested font size, margin size and spacing, and contact the school's admissions office for clarification if necessary.

# Putting It All Together

To help illustrate how the entire essay writing process comes together, in this section, we apply the lessons and guidelines from the Essay Outlining chap-

Essay Writing

ter and from this chapter and create an essay from scratch. We will work with the following essay question:

**Give us an example of a situation in which you displayed leadership. What did you learn from your experience? (500-word maximum)**

In this case, the experience to be discussed will be a story about establishing a charitable program at a hospital. Our first step, then, is to contemplate the story's central conflict and create a super summary for the essay.

Conflict: *When I tried to initiate a charitable program at the hospital that treated my mother, I was met with opposition from the hospital's director.*

Super Summary: *"Relying on my ability to think entrepreneurially and creatively, I was able to overcome obstacles and create an enduring program to aid the families of those suffering from cancer."*

Paragraph 1: Introduction to the situation and the concept (Introduction)

Paragraph 2: Establishment of the program and discovery of the resistance to it (Rising action)

Paragraph 3: Steps taken to address issues and overcome resistance (Rising action)

Paragraph 4: Success in implementation (Climax)

Paragraph 5: Lessons learned ("Takeaways") (Falling action/Conclusion)

With these major themes identified, we can now add the details that will bring each section—and the narrative as a whole—to life.

Paragraph 1: Introduction to the situation and the concept (Introduction)

- Description of the crisis situation
- Description of the touching gesture

Paragraph 2: Establishment of the program and discovery of the resistance to it (Rising action)

- Approaching the director with the concept
- Description of the concept
- Shock at rejection of the concept and the reasons given

Paragraph 3: Steps taken to address issues and overcome resistance (Rising action)

- Fairness: Expanded the program
- Cost: Ensured families would commit to picking up the costs
- Confidentiality: Solicited help of Web designer and lawyer pro bono

Paragraph 4: Success in implementation (Climax)

- Delivered an almost live program to director
- Earned right to launch and see what would happen
- Saw program succeed

Paragraph 5: Lessons learned ("Takeaways") (Falling action/Conclusion)

- May have been a bit naïve about her immediate acceptance
- Entrepreneurial, determined, passionate

The final step in conceptualizing the essay is setting the tone with an interesting opening line. For this essay, we will use a "maintaining the mystery" opening to create a visual and not immediately reveal too much. The entire sample essay follows:

*Trays of lasagna. Bowls of salad. Plates of freshly cut fruit.[1] When I returned one day from visiting my mother at the hospital, I was surprised to find that our friends had gotten together to make us homemade meals, so that my father, siblings and I could focus on our mother, not on time-consuming but essential tasks like cooking. I could not help but think, "What if others do not have this kind of support system? Who helps to ease their burden and take care of them?"[2]*

*Months after my mother's battle with cancer ended,[3] I called the director of St. John's Hospital to propose a program, wherein volunteers from one family would assume the costs of and deliver meals to another during a critical family illness. I was surprised by the director's knee-jerk rejection of my idea, citing fairness ("not all families would be served"), privacy issues and— despite my assurances—costs as reasons she was "unenthusiastic" about what I felt was a crucial program.[4]*

*Frustrated, I went to work addressing her critiques. With respect to fairness, she left me only one choice: expand the program. I had already assembled a list of 25 volunteer families and quickly sent out an email asking them to suggest friends. I created a Twitter feed and a Facebook page where I announced (with permission) each new volunteer family, as did the new volunteers themselves, creating a viral effect. In three days, I signed up 30 more volunteer families, all of whom agreed to pay for the food they would prepare. While scanning the list of volunteers, I noticed a prominent lawyer, whom I approached to develop confidentiality agreements on a pro-bono basis. I then asked a graphic designer on the list to*

---

1 With this introduction, an image is evoked, which is more appealing and captivating than a direct statement like "I was fortunate to have a team of friends making sure we had ample food in our home during the time of my mother's illness" would be.

2 This is not an overt thesis, but a subtle nod to the direction the story will take. It gives the reader "credit"—he/she will "get it" without it being explicitly presented.

3 The health of the individual's mother is not truly central to the story. Thus, the individual leaves her condition unresolved, keeping the reader focused on his actions instead.

4 Here, in the rising action, we see the conflict beginning to emerge: the protagonist is at odds with the director, creating the tension that the reader wants to see resolved.

*create a basic Web site where volunteers could enroll in the program, commit to covering the costs involved and sign confidentiality agreements.[5]*

*When I returned to see the director, I did so not with an idea, but with a functioning program in hand. With my list of enthusiastic chefs, who had signed confidentiality agreements and committed to paying for the meals, in hand, I went through our site with her. "How can I say no?" she said, shaking her head in disbelief. "Let's give it a shot."[6] That weekend, we delivered our first meals and were met with smiles, hugs and tears. Today, we have more than 150 volunteer families, each committed to cooking four times per year, and dozens of families being cared for throughout our city each weekend.[7]*

*It is immensely gratifying to see this program "live," but I look back and recognize that I may have been blinded by my own idea and thus did not anticipate the challenges involved. Still, calling on my entrepreneurial spirit, I persisted and acted decisively and resourcefully to alleviate each of the director's concerns and set the program up to succeed. In the end, my ability to implement matched the level of my passion, allowing us all to deliver quite meaningfully.[8]*

# Additional Sample Narrative Essay

The following narrative essay, written by mbaMission Founder and President Jeremy Shinewald, was published in the award-winning Canadian monthly magazine *The Walrus* in December 2006. Although this narrative was not composed as a response to a business school essay question, it stands as a worthwhile example of the tenets of narrative writing extolled in this chapter.

---

5  The rising action continues here, building toward the climax. What will happen? Will these actions pay off, or will the protagonist be disappointed again?

6  The story reaches its climax with the formerly disappointed protagonist redeemed and the director redeemed as well.

7  In the brief falling action here, the program itself is validated, increasing the legitimacy of the protagonist's idea and actions.

8  In this thoughtful conclusion, the protagonist is honest about his strengths and weaknesses, which allows him to connect with the reader.

Come on Down! A Winnipeg Boy Waits for the Payoff on *The Price is Right*

*When I arrive at the CBS studios at 5:10 a.m. on an unremarkable Tuesday in April, there are over a hundred others in line, the most zealous of whom arrived last night. Amid the darkness and frigid temperatures, dozens of hopefuls lie on the sidewalk in sleeping bags and blankets, while others sit mummified in lawn chairs, waiting patiently for the gates of the compound to swing open. This is my competition. Who among us will stand triumphant on the glitter-dipped stage of the longest-running game show in television history?*

*Stephen, a burly engineer with Frito-Lay, and his wife, Kelly, a blond, blue-eyed cashier, tell me they drove all the way from Phoenix to attend yesterday's taping and rue what they believe was a near miss. "I was so sure the producers were going to pick him," Kelly says. "They kept asking Stephen questions, and he had them laughing," she adds, confirming what I learned from someone who once made it to the Showcase Showdown: it only appears that contestants are chosen at random. In fact, producers pre-select audience members who promise to make the show a high-energy affair.*

*Behind me in line may be just such a character. Bill, a cherubic retiree from Utah, jumps up and down on the spot while explaining that he's prepared to deal with the cold if it means a chance to stand face to face with Bob Barker, "a real gentleman" and "class act." As the sun rises, people around me shed their blankets and sweatshirts, revealing homemade T-shirts with attention-getting slogans such as "Bob is a Stud" and "Barker's Other Beauties." I'm clearly behind the eight ball in my generic* Price is Right *shirt, hastily purchased from the CBS gift shop.*

*I soon discover another possible disadvantage—I haven't studied. Connie, a "second-generation fan" (her mother won a trip to France in the 1970s), has been TiVoing the show for six months and has created a* price list of every item they've featured, from toaster ovens to decorative Ionic columns. Her son glances up from his Bible to offer me some useful advice: "If you get up on stage, look for my mom. She knows every price."

Around noon, the line finally starts to snake toward the producers. "What's your name and where are you from?" they ask one potential contestant after another. When they come to Stephen, however, it's "Nice to have you back." I'm sure he's a shoo-in. I'm next, so I pull myself together and try to project "high energy," shouting, "I travelled 1,400 miles from Winnipeg, Canada, to hear those famous words, 'Jeremy Shinewald, come on down! You're the next contestant on The Price is Right!'" "You and 300 other people," the producer quips, but I sense this is a test and laugh along with him. Will it be enough?

The screaming begins the moment we enter the studio, ratcheting up a notch when a handful of audience members are invited onstage to dance. Seventy-something Anne is soon on her feet, gently rocking back and forth and snapping her fingers, unfazed by the frat boy who is leaning back on one hand and thrusting his pelvis toward her. By the time Bob appears, the crowd is in hysterics. Stephen is the third person called to "come on down!" He wins the first item up for bid (a set of his-and-hers bicycles), which earns him a shot at a game of "Clearance Sale" and, later, a turn at the money wheel. There, he spins himself $6,000 and one of two places in the vaunted Showcase Showdown. Kelly clasps her hands and cries tears of joy.

As I watch contestant after contestant running down the aisles, my own chances growing slimmer and slimmer, I am overcome by self-doubt. Maybe I was too enthusiastic with the producers. Maybe I should return the next day to show them how serious I am. But am I that serious after all? Perhaps I'm just not Price is Right material. And then a higher power intervenes: "Jeremy Shinewald, come on down! You're the next contes-

*tant on The Price is Right!" Suddenly, I am racing down the aisle, past Stephen's empty seat, past Kelly, Bill, and Anne, high-fiving strangers.*

*I turn to look for Connie as soon as I reach Contestants' Row. Announcer Rich Fields delivers the marketing pitch for a set of eight VTech phones, and Bob asks me for my bid. As I desperately scan the audience, Bob starts to badger me: "How about a bid, Jeremy?" I still can't find Connie. "Jeremy?" Finally, I spot her and, amid the deafening noise, try to follow her hand signals. She's holding six fingers in the air and pumping them vigorously in my direction. Is it $660? $600? I can't think. "$650!" The other contestants give their bids, and we turn to Bob for the verdict. "Actual retail price, six hundred . . . "— I start to raise my arms in victory—". . . and ten dollars. The winner is Jamie!"*

*Jamie, whose bid of $475 comes closest to the retail price without going over (though it is technically less accurate than mine), skips to the stage, cheered on by her sorority sisters. Humbled, I watch the rest of the show from Contestants' Row. Stephen wins his $26,937 showcase, which includes a set of boxing equipment, three kitchen appliances, and a Pontiac Grand Am GT Coupe. Naturally, Kelly joins him on stage for the big finale. Then, to my surprise, Stephen calls me up too, which is how I come to stand in front of America, beside Bob and his Beauties, hugging a virtual stranger and his wife as they live what seems to be their happiest moment.*

*The theme music dies and I am whisked offstage, where I'm prodded to sign a release form giving up all commercial rights to the show. I receive an 8 x 10 glossy of Bob holding a poodle, along with instructions on how to claim my parting gifts: an electric wheelbarrow and a wine-bottle opener. When the paperwork is completed, an usher escorts me to a door through which I am to rejoin the world of mortals. From the darkness of the stairwell, I step out into the beyond, forbidden to ever return to Contestants' Row.*

# Resume

· · · · · · · · · · · · · · · · · · · · · · · ·

## Chapter 4

# *Resume*

In revising your resume to be submitted with your business school application, your overall goal is to create a document that showcases your major accomplishments and career progress for the admissions committee in an effective and compelling way. The advice provided in this guide will help you achieve that goal.

Many MBA candidates will focus intensively on their essays and prepare endlessly for their interviews, but will merely submit the most recent professional resume that that they have on file, all but ignoring the opportunity to make a statement about themselves. Your resume is not a "throwaway" but rather an opportunity to tell your professional and even your personal story in a concise form. So, you should ensure that your resume is constructed for maximum impact, while still meeting the specific expectations of your target school's admissions committee. Your goal should be to create a resume that is simple and consistent in style while also brief and powerful in substance.

## Space Concerns

Ideally, your resume should be only one page long; admissions committees generally expect and appreciate the conciseness of this format. If you choose to submit a two-page resume or longer, the reader may have difficulty scanning it and identifying (and remembering) important facts. With these space constraints in mind, we offer two fairly straightforward "space saver" ideas:

1) Do not include a mission statement at the beginning of your resume. Your mission in this case is to get into the MBA program to which you are applying—and, of course, the admissions committee already knows this! A mission statement will take up precious space that can be used more effectively for other purposes.

2) Only your name should appear at the top of your resume. You do not need to include your address, email address, gender, marital status, etc., because this data will all be provided in your application form. As with a mission statement, adding this kind of information will take up precious space that can be used more effectively for other purposes.

As you construct your resume, you will create headings and sections for the different kinds of information covered within it—Professional Experience, Education, Military Experience, Entrepreneurial Experience, Community Work, Personal, Leadership and more. Although we generally recommend that you limit your headings to only those that are the most relevant and important to your life experiences, headings serve to bring special attention to the unique aspects of your resume and establish a framework for a chronology that could otherwise be confusing. So, for example, if you have been working as an accountant and also founded a start-up on the side and the dates of these experiences overlap, you may want to create a separate Entrepreneurial Experience section to distinguish and highlight these accomplishments individually. Doing so gives the reader the cue that one experience was traditional and the other was "extracurricular." A resume is like a map of your career, and you want the reader to be able to navigate that map as easily as possible.

## Structuring Your Entries

Each major entry beneath these headings typically begins with employer and job title for professional positions or your university and degree for academic accomplishments and should be distinguished with larger font and/or bold type. (Avoid underlining anything in a resume, because this can clutter the page.) MBA programs are most interested in candidates' professional lives, so, almost always—except, perhaps, when the applicant has recently completed cutting-edge research at the Master's or Ph.D. level—candidates should list their professional experiences before they offer their academic experiences.

Then, use bullet points within each entry to organize and present information clearly, as illustrated in the following example:

| 2002–2004 | **XYZ Technologies, Inc.** | Chicago, Illinois |

**Business Development Manager**

*XYZ is a 17-employee, venture-funded, video-software start-up.*

- Established software-bundling relationships with Moonvideo and Audio4, resulting in $1M in new revenue, representing 30% of total firm revenue.

- Managed group of six web developers, three graphic designers and three copywriters in New York City and Beijing, completing specialized product launch Web site on time and under budget.

Typically, you should list your company name first and then your title with each entry, but use your judgment when deciding how to structure your particular resume. For example, if you have held several positions with a single company, the company name should appear only once, with multiple positions listed beneath. Many candidates mistakenly choose to list only their most recent position with their firm and lump all their accomplishments under this final role, even those achieved in previous positions with the company. Unfortunately, such an approach deprives the reader of the visual cues that reveal promotions. Consider the differences between the two following simplified examples. In the first, the reader is given no indication that the MBA candidate has earned two promotions while with the firm. In the second, the individual's growth should be quite clear.

Resume

*Example A*:

2004–Present  **Mercury Manufacturing**              Detroit, Michigan

*Mercury is a $43M manufacturing company specializing in automotive parts.*

**Manager, International Purchasing**

• Managed seven-person staff to troubleshoot internal supply-chain inefficiencies, reducing costs by 17%.

• Determined supplier qualification criteria, training all senior purchasing staff members to accept/reject supplier bids and determine "preferred supplier" status.

• Conducted due diligence on 15 potential suppliers; presented "green light" recommendations to senior management on seven firms, all of which were accepted.

*Example B*:

2004–Present  **Mercury Manufacturing**              Detroit, Michigan

*Mercury is a $43M manufacturing company specializing in automotive parts.*

2008–Present  **Manager, International Purchasing**

• Managed seven-person staff to troubleshoot internal supply-chain inefficiencies, reducing costs by 17%.

2006–2008  **Associate, International Purchasing**

• Determined supplier qualification criteria, training all senior purchasing staff members to accept/reject supplier bids and determine "preferred supplier" status.

2004–2006     **Analyst, International Acquisitions**

- Conducted due diligence on 15 potential suppliers; presented "green light" recommendations to senior management on seven firms, all of which were accepted.

# Showcasing Your Accomplishments

As you may have noticed in our sample entries thus far, you should use bullet points to *showcase your accomplishments*, not merely state responsibilities. When only your responsibilities are presented—with no accompanying results—the reader has no understanding of whether you were effective in your position. For example, consider the following entry, in which only responsibilities are offered:

2005–Present     **Household Products Group, Flocter & Gramble**    Cincinnati, Ohio

**Brand Manager**

- Responsible for managing a $10M media campaign, supervising a staff of five junior brand managers, monitoring daily sales volumes and ensuring the consistent supply of product from five production facilities in three countries.

The reader is left wondering, "Was the media campaign successful? Did the staff of five progress? Did sales volumes increase? Did the supply of products reach its destination?" When this one large bullet point is instead broken down into individual bulleted entries that elaborate on each task and show clear results, the reader learns not just about the candidate's responsibilities, but also about his/her effectiveness and successes.

Resume

| 2008–Present | **Flocter & Gramble** | Cincinnati, Ohio |
| | **Brand Manager** | |

- Initiated $10M television/Internet "Island Vacation" promotion introducing new Shine brand detergent, surpassing first-year sales targets within three months.

- Mentored and supervised five Junior Brand Managers, each of whom was promoted to Brand Manager (company traditionally promotes 25%).

- Analyzed daily sales volumes and identified opportunity to increase price point in Midwest, resulting in 26% margin improvement and $35M in new profits.

- Secured "safety supply" of vital chemicals from alternative suppliers, ensuring 99% order fulfillment.

By comparing the first Flocter & Gramble entry with the second, you can see how much more effective an accomplishment-driven resume is than one that simply states responsibilities.

You may have noticed that each bullet point in the second Flocter & Gramble sample entry begins with an action-oriented verb: *initiated, mentored, analyzed, secured.* Such verbs, which indicate deliberate, focused action, make a stronger impact on the reader. You should take care to avoid words that may make your contributions seem vague or even ineffectual, as in the following examples:

- Helped team achieve target goals (*How did you help?*)

- Contributed to strategic planning meetings (*How did you contribute?*)

Words such as *helped* and *contributed* do not convey what you accomplished and thus do not promote you as someone who leads and gets things done. (Consult the list of action-oriented verbs provided later in this chapter for assistance in choosing words that will bolster your resume entries' effectiveness.) If you lead with action-oriented verbs and close with quantifiable results, you should have strong bullet points throughout your resume. However, you may be asking yourself, "What if my results are not quantifiable?"

While quantifiable results are preferred because they clearly convey your success in the actions you undertook, in some instances, you simply cannot quantify your success. In such cases, you might instead demonstrate non-quantifiable or even potential results. Consider the following examples:

- Persuaded management to review existing operations; currently leading Manufacturing Review Committee, which will submit its final report in June 2012.

- Established divisional continuing education series, noted on review as "crucial" and "game changing."

- Initiated biweekly "Tuesday at Five" team social event, resulting in enhanced workplace morale.

In each of these sample bullets, the results are not measurable, but they are nonetheless important. Although the results of the Manufacturing Committee Review are not yet known, the reader knows that management is taking the operations review seriously because a deadline has been set and the report results are anticipated. One cannot really quantify the impact of the divisional educational series, but the reader understands that the MBA candidate was effective and influential, based on the feedback he/she received. Admittedly, the final result of these actions is vague and depends on individual judgment, yet the outcome of the "Tuesdays at Five" initiative, by contrast, can indeed be qualified in some way. The accomplishment, while "soft," is clearly positive.

Be sure to include any special acknowledgements or awards you may have received at work, and explain their criteria, as in the following example:

Resume

- Received "High Performer" award, given to the top 3% of all Brand Managers, based on sales, profits and a 360-degree review.

Similarly, you should list awards/honors, club or team involvement, publications, community work, etc., from your academic career in the Education section (or whichever section makes most sense). Indicate the results of your activities/efforts, whenever possible.

Your resume should not necessarily list every one of your accomplishments in a specific position but instead should showcase only those that are most impressive. Further, the emphasis in your resume should be on current and recent positions. In general, you should aim to have more bullet points (i.e., five to six) for current and recent positions and fewer (i.e., three to four) for those positions you held much earlier in your career. However, if your current or most recent position was very short in tenure and your earlier roles were more lengthy, your dispersement of bullets may differ, with fewer for the later positions and more for the earlier ones.

Perhaps surprisingly, you do not necessarily have to list every professional position you have held thus far in your career. Positions that are six or seven years old may not offer any useful or currently relevant information about you, and they may not add to your profile (e.g., indicating that you worked in marketing for six months in 2001 may not be useful if you then spent the next four years in consulting). Some candidates with more professional experience may want to consider omitting internships and/or other quasi-professional experiences in some instances. However, omitting a potential resume entry requires judgment! Proceed with common sense and prudence, and if you are working with an mbaMission consultant, consider asking his/her advice on the entry.

If you worked for a company that you believe is not readily recognizable to most people, offer a brief description of the firm *in italics*. Although many companies, and especially large and international ones, are known by most admissions committee readers, you cannot expect that everyone will be familiar with every company on your resume. Including a company description will also allow you to emphasize the aspects of the company that cast your accomplishments in a better light. Consider the following example:

| | | |
|---|---|---|
| 2002–2004 | **XYZ Technologies, Inc.** | Chicago, Illinois |

*XYZ is a 17-employee, venture-funded, video-software start-up.*

# Special Sections

## Personal

Provide a brief Personal section at the end of your resume, in which you list interests, hobbies and community activities. As with all other entries, include accomplishments for the items in this section wherever possible. A Personal section provides another opportunity for you to demonstrate your ability to lead, to highlight non-work accomplishments and to showcase your personal passions. This kind of information also helps to humanize you in the admissions committee's eyes and, in some cases, can even reveal common ground— "You ran the New York City Marathon in 2005? I ran it in 2009!"—which can be especially useful in an interview.

Moreover, be specific about your interests. For example, writing "Restoring 1960s Jaguar E-type coupes" carries more of an impact than simply "Restoring cars," and also gives the reader more personalized information with which to evaluate you. Although you should always be careful to exercise restraint in this section, listing attention-getting interests such as steeplechasing or playing bagpipes (as long as you are truthful!) can really make your resume stand out. Note that your resume should not list basic computer skills; such proficiencies are expected today, and listing them will take up precious space that could be used more effectively for other purposes.

Resume

## Leadership

Some candidates choose to include a separate Leadership section in their resume in which to highlight leadership activities. Doing so is fine if the following are true:

- You have significant leadership activities tied to noticeable achievements that you want to highlight and that will not come across as clearly in a more general (and more brief) Personal section.

- Incorporating such a section will not detract substantially from the listings in your Experience section. Leadership activities should complement—never replace—substantive work accomplishments.

- Your leadership experiences highlight something different about you, revealing you to be a more well-rounded candidate. For example, if you work in investment banking and have spent several years coaching inner-city kids in tennis, you might choose to highlight your role as a coach in a separate Leadership section.

# Formatting

Take care to be consistent with punctuation and style. If you want to have periods at the end of each bullet point, go ahead. If you prefer not having periods, that is also fine. However, you must be consistent, or your resume will look sloppy. This same guideline applies to indentation, capitalization, use of bolding and italics, and so on.

Using effective formatting to make your resume's appearance more appealing and your content more compelling is an important step and one that requires attention to certain guidelines. First, avoid common design errors, such as making your margins too narrow, trying to fit too much information onto the page (often by making the font too small to be easily read), not leaving enough white space and overemphasizing field headings (Experience, Education, etc.). Your resume should be structured such that any reader can easily find his/her way around the document even if field headings were left out.

Second, use emphasis tools—such as boldface, enlarged typeface and surrounding white space—to accentuate only the most important parts of your resume. Excessive use of these tools blunts their effect and dilutes their impact. Thus, reserve the use of emphasis tools to draw attention to such elements as your name, dates, company names and job titles. Also, be consistent in your use of emphasis tools throughout the document. Ideally, the reader should be able to blur his/her eyes and still be able to locate and identify the major sections of the document.

Take care to ensure that your resume reflects and supports your life story and personal statement as they are presented in your essays and other parts of your application. If you assert in your personal statement that you have always hoped to someday run your own business, for example, then be sure to emphasize in your resume the entrepreneurial aspects of your professional experiences to date. You may also want to highlight any facets of your life outside work that have an entrepreneurial element in the Personal section of your resume or, if substantial, in a separate Entrepreneurial Experience section. And of course, list any leadership roles you have held as part of your volunteer activities.

Resume

# Consulting and Investment Banking Resumes

If you have worked as a consultant or in any other kind of environment or role that centers on project work, list your most important undertakings and related accomplishments after the company name and job title, preceded by the words "Representative project work includes the following:". If you are not comfortable listing the names of your clients (or are not authorized to do so), give a short description of the client instead, such as "$125M Germany-based machine tool manufacturer." A similar approach can be used by bankers to detail representative transactions on which they have worked.

| 2008–Present | **Hughes Allan Hamilton** | Chicago, Illinois |

**Manager, Northeast Region Financial Services Group**

Representative project work includes the following:

- Top-five publicly traded insurance company—retooled information systems. Analyzed the business and technology strategy and recommended alternative migration strategies, resulting in a 20% cost reduction.

- $15B manufacturer of consumer products—led a team that identified business process improvements for the item processing operations. Completed a detailed cost/benefit analysis that resulted in $5M in annual savings.

If possible, submit your finalized resume in .pdf format. Doing so will ensure that the document will have a much more attractive presentation on screen and also prevents any formatting problems that might otherwise result from printer incompatibility, a mismatch in word processor versions or the use of fonts that are not available on the reader's computer. Be sure to double-check your resume one last time in .pdf format, in case anything went wrong during the conversion from your word-processing program. The best way to do this check is to print the .pdf file out on paper. Avoid proofreading on a computer screen; you're likely to miss the errors.

We have included several sample resumes on the following pages.

Resume

# John A. Macdonald[1]

## Experience

2009–Present    **Flocter & Gramble**            Cincinnati, Ohio
**Brand Manager**

- Initiated $10M television/Internet "Island Vacation" promotion to introduce new Shine brand detergent; surpassed first year's sales targets in three months.
- Mentored and supervised five junior brand managers, each of whom was promoted to brand manager (company traditionally promotes 25%).
- Analyzed daily sales volumes and identified opportunity to increase price point in Midwest, resulting in a 26% margin improvement and $35M in new profits.[2]
- Secured "safe supply" of vital chemical components from alternative suppliers, ensuring 99% order fulfillment.
- Persuaded management to review existing operations; currently leading Manufacturing Review Committee, which will table its final report in June 2012.
- Received "High Performer" award, given to the top 3% of all Brand Managers, based on sales, profits and a 360-degree review.

2007–2009    **XYZ Technologies, Inc.**           Chicago, Illinois
*XYZ is a 17-employee, venture-funded, video-software start-up.*[3]
**Business Development Manager**

- Established software-bundling relationships with Moonvideo and Audio4, resulting in $1M in new revenue, representing 30% of total firm revenue.
- Managed group of six Web developers, three graphic designers and three copywriters in New York City and Beijing,[4] completing specialized product launch Web site on time and under budget.
- Created and chaired industry trade group (Independent Video-Software Producers), successfully lobbying for XYZ products as the standard for the market.

---

1 Only the name is needed here. Notice how the larger font and surrounding white space really make the name stand out. Be careful of using too much emphasis in the document, and limit such use to your name, position titles, company names and university names.

2 Be as quantitative as possible when listing your accomplishments. Numbers have far greater impact than adjectives. This is especially important with positions of this kind, in which the responsibilities brand managers hold can vary widely across companies.

3 Be sure to include a company description if the company is not commonly known.

4 Whenever possible, list the number and titles of direct reports. Doing so offers insight into how substantial your job is/was. Titles like vice president and director are often given to people who have no reports at all.

| Summer 2006 | **FCB Public Relations, Inc.** | Tokyo, Japan |
| | **Public Relations Intern** | |

*FCB is a boutique public relations firm with offices in Tokyo and Seattle.*

- Led Japanese consumer products firm through internal branding development exercises, creating new employee retention strategy.
- Designed surveys and identified more than 400 respondents, completing market research that drove the launch of a new Japanese food product.

## Education

| 2006 | **University of ABC** | Cleveland, Ohio |
| | **Bachelor of Arts—Economics, Honors** | |

- Dean's Honor List (Top 5% of Class),[5] 2004, 2005, 2006.
- Captain, NCAA Division I Swimming Team, 2002–2006.[6]
- Treasurer, ABC Student Government; managed $200,000 in student funds.
- Publication, *Interest Rate Fluctuations in Canada*, Cambridge Press, 2005.[7]

## Personal

**Community**: Big Brother, 2008–Present.
**Languages**: Swahili (near fluency), French (proficient), Japanese (basic).[8]
**Interests**: Play ice hockey three times a week; enjoy Japanese cooking; have travelled to 27 countries.

---

5  When applicable, and if space allows, disclose the criteria for an award or honor if you believe doing so will increase the achievement's impact.

6  Athletic accomplishments, especially those that include a leadership role (as this one does), can be helpful, because both admissions committees and employers often see such activities/roles as a reflection of hard work and strong character.

7  Publications, elected positions and awards reflect the high esteem others hold for you and can often be more impressive in the reader's eyes than self-reported accomplishments.

8  Listing language proficiency not only reveals your range of abilities in this area, but can also reflect positively on your work ethic and character.

# Patricia Johnson

Experience

2008–Present **Hughes Allan Hamilton** Chicago, Illinois
**Manager, Southeast Region Financial Services Group**

Representative project work includes the following:[1]
- Top-five publicly traded insurance company – retooled information systems. Analyzed the business and technology strategy and recommended alternative migration strategies, resulting in a 20% cost reduction.
- $15B manufacturer of consumer products – led a team that identified business process improvements for the item processing operations. Completed a detailed cost/benefit analysis that resulted in $5M in annual savings.

2005–2008 **Senior Consultant**[2]

Representative project work includes the following:
- Top-ten North American commercial bank[3]—compiled business requirements into systems design for a custom investment management system, resulting in a 24% reduction in system costs.
- Top-five privately held insurance company—evaluated business requirements for a universal life system and selected platform systems for acquisition. Migration resulted in closing a redundant 75-person operation center and $11M in annual savings.
- Top-five North American commercial bank – translated business requirements into systems design, resulting in an 11% reduction in the time from application to funding and a substantial increase in capacity.

2003–2005 **Staff Consultant**

Representative project work includes the following:
- Commonwealth Edison[4]—designed and programmed department cost system, implemented on time and on budget.

---

1 For banking and consulting resumes, the use of the "representative project work" or "representative transactions" approach highlights the most substantial accomplishments while leaving the door open to discuss other experiences during an interview.
2 While you may be tempted to leave out earlier titles, be careful. Skillful resume readers know that rapid promotions speak volumes about a person's skills and abilities in a way that self-reported accomplishments do not.
3 To maintain confidentiality, you can "mask" your client engagements. The admissions committees have seen it all and understand such things.
4 Consider using the actual name of the company for which you consulted if (1) you are comfortable and/or authorized to do so, (2) the name is well known and (3) you think it will make the accomplishment more impressive. Otherwise, a short company description may have a greater impact.

Resume

- Arizona Department of Transportation – designed and programmed a custom revenue tracking system, leading to a 27% decrease in administrative costs in the first year of operation.

**Education**

2003  **University of QRS**                                    Orlando, Florida
Bachelor of Science, Mathematics; *Magna cum laude.*
Thesis: "Using Black-Scholes option valuations techniques to model flu outbreaks," published in *Applications Digest*, June 2003.

**Leadership**  **Head, Anchor Ball Planning Committee**, St. Clement Church School. Coordinated more than 85 volunteers and set a record for funds raised (over $250,000).[5]

**Coach, Lincoln Park High School girls soccer team.** Organized all events, coordinated transportation and oversaw practices, ultimately leading the team to win the county championship for the first time in school history.

**Personal**  Certified Financial Planner, 2006.
Racing sailboats (finished second in 2005 Mackinac); playing, coaching and refereeing soccer.

Resume

---

5  Including bullets under a community endeavor can be important in revealing accomplishment in addition to volunteer commitment. Too many MBA candidates list only the minimum information for such activities (organization/date), which means the reader remains unaware of anything of note that the candidate may have achieved.

# Matthew Wallace[1]

Experience

**Grocemania Corporation**                    Seattle, Washington

2008–Present   **Merchandise Planning Manager—Electronics Division**
- Led the planning and execution of $1B of annual product distribution and inventory control, achieving $20M in average inventory savings compared with plan.
- Managed and coached 12-person inventory team to negotiate shorter lead times with vendors, resulting in $30M reduction in working capital demands.
- Emphasized team career development; mentored and provided feedback and recognition; as a result, five team members have received promotions.
- Received "Flawless Execution" award, given to top 5% of all division members based on outstanding inventory control and minimized markdowns.
- Led division's 2009 United Way Fundraising Campaign, increasing donations by 7% over previous year.[2]

2005–2007   **Buyer—Outdoor Living Division**
- Developed creative merchandise assortments and new "exclusive" strategies for $200M division; surpassed sales goal by $25M and surpassed gross margin goal by $7.5M.
- Received April 2007 President's Award (awarded to top 3% of employees firmwide) for leadership in developing and launching an internal generic fertilizer brand. New line generated $14M in incremental sales in 2006.
- Developed cross-functional team of 20 to integrate marketing and finance divisions into category vision and growth; nominated for Collegiality Award.
- Initiated and chaired divisional green committee, reducing paper waste by 50% and division energy bill by 15%.

Resume

---

1  Notice the amount of white space here—and the improved readability—created by omitting the candidate's address and goal statement, both of which are unnecessary for this type of resume.
2  Although this accomplishment may not be core to the success of Grocemania as a business, it is certainly relevant in that it shows the candidate's diverse abilities and softer personal side.

## Education

2004        **State College of Western State**      Seattle, Washington

Bachelor of Arts, Marketing, with a concentration in Operations Management.

Treasurer, Faculty of Arts Student Body Council, 2003, 2004.

Student Nominee, Marketing Department Professor Hiring Panel, 2003.

## Leadership & Activities

2007–Present      Youth Sports Leader, River Heights Community Center

- Administered youth baseball league, supervising 10 umpires and 25 coaches across four age-groups.

2006–2009      Fundraising Volunteer, Special Olympics of Washington

- Raised $5,000 in sponsorship fees each year from local businesses.
- Identified and secured a national bronze sponsor, raising $25,000.

## Personal

Languages: Spanish (fluent), French (fluent).

Interests: Running (completed 2009 Boston Marathon), yoga (certified Bikram instructor), watching long-forgotten (and completely awful) B movies.[3]

Resume

---

3   Expressing a little flair and humor can be acceptable in the Personal section.

## List of Action-Oriented Verbs that Help Show
## Accomplishments, Rather than Responsibilities

| *A* | Arranged | *C* | Completed |
|---|---|---|---|
| Accelerated | Ascertained | Calculated | Composed |
| Accomplished | Assembled | Captured | Conceived |
| Achieved | Assessed | Cataloged | Conceptualized |
| Activated | Assigned | Centralized | Condensed |
| Adapted | Attained | Chaired | Conducted |
| Addressed | Augmented | Charted | Conferred |
| Adjusted | Authorized | Clarified | Conserved |
| Advanced | Awarded | Classified | Consolidated |
| Advocated | *B* | Coached | Constructed |
| Allocated | Balanced | Collaborated | Contacted |
| Answered | Boosted | Collected | Continued |
| Applied | Briefed | Combined | Controlled |
| Appraised | Budgeted | Communicated | Converted |
| Approved | Built | Compared | Convinced |
| Arbitrated | | Compiled | Coordinated |

Resume

| | | | |
|---|---|---|---|
| Corresponded | Diagnosed | Enhanced | **F** |
| Counseled | Directed | Enlarged | Fabricated |
| Created | Discovered | Enlisted | Facilitated |
| Critiqued | Displayed | Ensured | Fashioned |
| Cultivated | Distributed | Entertained | Finalized |
| Customized | Diverted | Established | Fixed |
| **D** | Documented | Estimated | Focused |
| Decided | Drafted | Evaluated | Forecasted |
| Defined | **E** | Examined | Formed |
| Delegated | Earned | Executed | Formulated |
| Delivered | Edited | Expanded | Fostered |
| Demonstrated | Educated | Expedited | Found |
| Designated | Eliminated | Experimented | Fulfilled |
| Designed | Emphasized | Explained | Furnished |
| Detected | Employed | Explored | **G** |
| Determined | Encouraged | Expressed | Gained |
| Developed | Enforced | Extended | Gathered |
| Devised | Engineered | Extracted | Generated |

Resume

| | | | |
|---|---|---|---|
| Governed | Increased | **J** | Mediated |
| Grossed | Influenced | Joined | Merged |
| Guided | Informed | Judged | Mobilized |
| **H** | Initiated | **L** | Modified |
| Handled | Innovated | Launched | Monitored |
| Headed | Inspected | Learned | Motivated |
| Heightened | Installed | Lectured | **N** |
| Hired | Instituted | Led | Navigated |
| Honed | Integrated | Lifted | Negotiated |
| Hosted | Interacted | Listened | Netted |
| **I** | Interpreted | Located | **O** |
| Identified | Interviewed | Logged | Obtained |
| Illustrated | Introduced | **M** | Opened |
| Imagined | Invented | Maintained | Operated |
| Implemented | Investigated | Managed | Ordered |
| Improved | Involved | Marketed | Orchestrated |
| Improvised | Issued | Maximized | Organized |
| Incorporated | | Measured | Originated |

| | | | |
|---|---|---|---|
| Outlined | Prevented | Ran | Reported |
| Overcame | Prioritized | Reached | Represented |
| Overhauled | Processed | Realized | Researched |
| Oversaw | Produced | Reasoned | Reshaped |
| **P** | Programmed | Received | Resolved |
| Performed | Projected | Recommended | Responded |
| Persuaded | Promoted | Reconciled | Restored |
| Pinpointed | Proposed | Recorded | Retrieved |
| Piloted | Protected | Recruited | Reviewed |
| Pioneered | Proved | Reduced | Revised |
| Placed | Provided | Referred | Revitalized |
| Planned | Publicized | Regulated | Routed |
| Played | Purchased | Rehabilitated | **S** |
| Predicted | **Q** | Related | Saved |
| Prepared | Qualified | Rendered | Screened |
| Prescribed | Questioned | Reorganized | Searched |
| Presented | **R** | Repaired | Secured |
| Presided | Raised | Replaced | Selected |

| | | | |
|---|---|---|---|
| Served | Strengthened | Trained | Verified |
| Shaped | Structured | Transcribed | Volunteered |
| Shared | Studied | Transformed | **W** |
| Simplified | Suggested | Transmitted | Weighed |
| Simulated | Summarized | Translated | Won |
| Sketched | Supervised | Tutored | Worked |
| Sold | Supplied | **U** | Wrote |
| Solved | Supported | Uncovered | |
| Sorted | Surpassed | Undertook | |
| Spearheaded | Surveyed | Unified | |
| Specialized | Sustained | United | |
| Specified | Synthesized | Updated | |
| Spoke | **T** | Upgraded | |
| Sponsored | Targeted | Used | |
| Staffed | Taught | Utilized | |
| Standardized | Tested | **V** | |
| Started | Tracked | Validated | |
| Streamlined | Traded | Verbalized | |

# Personal Statement

Chapter 5

# *Introduction*

Virtually all top business schools—with some notable exceptions—ask applicants for a personal statement in which candidates discuss their goals and ambitions as they pertain to the MBA degree and, often, to the target school's particular program. As you approach this essay, be sure that you place the appropriate emphasis on the "personal" aspect of what you plan to write, because you will need to take ownership of and truly tell *your* story in a way that is not only clear and compelling, but that also reveals your personality and individuality. You cannot afford to be generic or vague when stating your goals or the reasons why you want to attend a certain school. Instead, you must write with purpose and conviction to impress upon the admissions committee that you have maturity and vision and will see your goals through.

In practically all personal statements, you must discuss your past (work experience), present (need for an MBA and the school's ability to facilitate your academic and professional objectives) and future (career goals) with insight and focus. However, note that we actually recommend a *past, future, present* sequence for this essay, because in this case, the most logical approach is to first give context and background about yourself, next describe your goals and then explain why you need the particular school's resources to achieve those goals. Convincingly explaining why a school's resources are required to help you achieve your goals would be quite challenging if you have not first stated what those goals are.

Personal Statement

# Past: Context and Work Experience

In recent years, top MBA programs have been de-emphasizing work history to some degree in the personal statement. Most schools' personal statement essay questions used to read a lot like this: "Discuss your work history. Why do you need an MBA to achieve your goals? Why do you want an MBA from our program?" In conversations with admissions officers, mbaMission has come to understand that many felt that the resume, recommendations, other essays and interview provide sufficient information about a candidate's background and that a work history was increasingly unnecessary. Still, some personal statement questions follow this traditional approach, as is the case with Kellogg:

*Northwestern University (Kellogg): Briefly assess your career progress to date. Elaborate on your future career plans and your motivation for pursuing a graduate degree at Kellogg. (600-word limit; 2009–2010 essay question)*

Meanwhile, others—such as those for Columbia Business School and the University of Michigan (Ross), which follow—do not explicitly ask you to discuss past experiences, but providing some basic context for your goals is still important.

*Columbia Business School: What are your short-term and long-term post-MBA goals? How will Columbia Business School help you achieve these goals? (Recommended 750-word limit; 2009–2010 essay question)*

*University of Michigan (Ross): Briefly describe your short-term and long-term career goals. Why is an MBA the best choice at this point in your career? What and/or who influenced your decision to apply to Ross? (500-word maximum; 2009–2010 essay question)*

If a school explicitly asks you to discuss your "career progress to date," do not take this as an opportunity to offer every accomplishment on your resume.

Some candidates make the mistake of writing about their work experience for 75% of their personal statements, even though they are also submitting a resume with their application. This wastes precious essay space by repeating facts the admissions committee already has elsewhere. We recommend limiting your discussion of your career history to approximately 40% of the essay length and including brief, but strong, examples of success to represent an accomplished career.

When no explicit request is made for information about your past, you should still include some brief background to make your present and future goals relevant. For example, a statement such as "My long-term goal is to become director of marketing for a major league sports franchise" becomes much more reasonable—and the stated goal seems more attainable—when the candidate also offers information about his/her past experience in sports management. Context connects the past and the future. With questions like Columbia's and Ross's, candidates should limit their career history to 50–125 words—or approximately 10%–15% of the total allowed word count—of context, so the career goals are clearly plausible and connect to a broader story.

Admissions committees are much more interested in understanding the decisions you have made and the processes through which you have grown than reading a summary of your past work experiences. Indeed, the presentation of your career progress in your essay should show professional milestones and momentum toward your future career goals. Your career history in this context is not meant to be a full review of your professional past, but rather a story that leads the reader to understand and admire your future goals.

If you are a career changer, as many MBA candidates are, your work history may not seem to link as definitively with your stated goals, at least in comparison with someone who plans to continue working within the same industry or job function after business school. However, you still need to show growth and accomplishment and highlight capabilities and knowledge.

Personal Statement

Emphasize the aspects of your career to date that are most relevant to your future goals, either because they have served as good preparation for your new intended career, or because they have given you some transferable skills that will be relevant to that career.

# Future: Career Goals

Your career goals should have a logical connection (if not a professional connection) to your professional history. The general idea is quite simple:

$$past\ experience + present\ MBA =$$
$$future\ professional\ goals.$$

## Short-Term Goals

Your short-term career goals need to show very clear direction and purpose. Simply writing *"When I graduate I want to go into marketing"* or *"With my MBA, I will enter the field of consulting"* is not enough. What kind of marketing (i.e., consumer products, business to business, etc.)? What knowledge do you have of consulting, and why will you excel? Remember, this is not a statement of dreams, but a statement of purpose, so you need to provide far greater depth. As you develop your short-term goals, you must consider the specific role they will play in enabling you to attain your long-term goals. You should demonstrate why you will excel in pursuing your goals and, ideally, show insight into why the market might even need you. Consider the following example:

*Given my background as a wine journalist, I am well aware of the traditional aspects of the wine-making industry and recognize that many vintners are slow to adapt to modern manufacturing and marketing techniques. With my MBA from ABC University, I will have the specific entrepreneurial and operational skills necessary to develop a small vineyard and nurture it so that it realizes its full potential. I see myself in my first position after earning my MBA as the general manager of an antiquated vineyard in the ABC region, implementing operational efficiencies, accessing capital for growth and marketing a superior product nationally and even internationally.*

In this example, the writer connects his/her experience as a wine journalist to his/her future as a general manager at a vineyard. He/she identifies a specific role to play and even illustrates the logic behind this role, which is essentially "some vineyards desperately need professional management talent." The reader is therefore left with a clear understanding of where this applicant is going, why this applicant will succeed and even why this applicant is needed in this field.

## Avoid Generic Statements

Declaring "I want to be a banker" or "I want to be a consultant" without any further clarification simply is not sufficient—you must explain as specifically as possible what you envision yourself doing after business school. For example, within the consulting industry, you will find many different "types" of consultants: marketing consultants, operational consultants, strategy consultants, technology consultants, small business consultants—even admissions consultants! Thus, stating merely that you "want to be a consultant" will reveal that you have not done your homework and do not really understand your field of interest or your possible place within it.

In contrast, consider this short-term goal statement:

*After graduating from Tuck, I intend to join either the Performance Improvement Group at Bain and Company, specializing in turnaround strategy, or the Operations Group at BCG, focusing on Rigorous Program Improvement.*

Personal Statement

Although this sentence is out of context, no one who reads it could credibly argue that the writer does not have a clear sense of purpose or knowledge of the consulting field.

In short, the admissions committee needs to see conviction and passion for a path; no business school that requests a goal statement is going to accept applicants who are unfocused with regard to why they want an MBA. However, conviction does not need to mean rigidity. Spend some time thinking through your goals very carefully. If you are not able to pinpoint an exact choice—or if you can envision more than one feasible route to your goal—under certain circumstances, offering alternatives for your short-term goals can be acceptable. (Note, of course, that alternate paths still need to involve a logical connection from past to present to future.) Consider the following example of offering alternative goals:

*In the long term, I would like to head a nonprofit organization that focuses on offering career guidance to inner-city high school students. I see two possible paths for achieving this goal. In the short term, I could work at a nonprofit with a similar mission, such as the Youngest Professionals Organization, working my way up and gaining concrete experience in managing a nonprofit. Or I could take a slightly different angle, working at Honesty Corporation, which targets its products to inner-city youth, to gain a better understanding of that population before moving from the business sector to the nonprofit one.*

Someone reading this statement should clearly see that the applicant is indeed quite serious about his/her long-term goals—so much so that he/she can envision at least two feasible routes toward them. Again, admissions committees want to understand that you are resolved about your future plans and view earning your MBA as a vital step in the right direction. Sometimes, maintaining perspective and offering a second possible path can reinforce that determination.

# Long-Term Goals

When proposing your long-term goal to the admissions committee, first keep in mind that you will need to demonstrate a cause and effect relationship between it and your short-term goal. Note also that long-term goals can be less specific than short-term goals—they essentially represent an ideal aspiration. While specificity is recommended for statements of short-term goals, admissions committees understand that no one can truly predict the future, so your long-term goals almost by necessity need to be less detailed. However, they should still clearly denote an intended and attainable career trajectory, as shown in the following example (which continues from the one offered in the Short-Term Goals section):

*In the long term, I would build on the success of this endeavor and would source and acquire multiple vineyards in need of modernization. Ultimately, I see my role in the firm as one of a portfolio manager, actively managing several vineyards and making decisions about capital allocation while leveraging operational and marketing efficiencies.*

## Avoid Unconnected Long- and Short-Term Goals

As stated, you must be sure to demonstrate a cause and effect relationship between your short- and long-term goals. While your goals can and should be whatever you desire for yourself (admissions committees do not have a "right" goal in mind that they expect from candidates) and may even seem quite disconnected from each other at first glance, this is fine as long as a causal connection exists—and is shown—between your short-term goals and your long-term goals. After all, your long-term goals are based on the assumption that your stated short-term goals will be reached; the positions you will hold later in your career will be facilitated by those you hold earlier.

For example, a statement such as "*In the short term, I want to be in marketing and in the long term, I want to become a banker*" would present a significantly

Personal Statement

disjointed transition—one that would likely perplex an admissions officer or career services advisor who reads it. Most short- and long-term goals can connect in some way. Equity research can be a foundation for consulting, for example, and marketing can be a basis for entrepreneurship. Generally, the goals themselves are not that relevant—the rationale behind these goals is what is vital. If the goals are well connected, they will be "real."

Moreover, given that these are your personal goals and part of your vision for your career and life, you most likely already know how they connect for you. The key is clearly communicating for the admissions reader how the transition you envision from your earlier role to your later one will play out in your post-MBA years.

## Avoid Disingenuous Goal Statements

Rather than expressing their sincere desires, some candidates make up goals they think the admissions committee wants to hear. These applicants tend to believe that the school is seeking only certain types of candidates who plan to pursue specific industries and positions, so they must fit this mold to gain acceptance to the MBA program. Not only is this untrue, but trying to guess what an admissions committee wants to hear and deliver it is also a recipe for failure. The end result is uninformed goals that lack context and sincerity. And considering that all parts of a candidate's application package should support the same career vision—including one's interview with the school, if applicable—presenting false goals here can jeopardize the applicant's entire candidacy.

Expressing what you truly feel and want to pursue is key. No amount of sophisticated language can make up for a lack of passion. Remember that admissions readers see thousands of essays every year—they are extremely experienced and can therefore tell when a candidate is being sincere and when he/she is just trying to say the "right" thing. Besides, writing the truth is not just more effective, it is also much easier.

# Present: Why *Our* MBA?

Perhaps above all else, schools want to hear very compelling reasons for each candidate's need for their particular program's MBA. Even when a school asks the generic question "Why do you need an MBA to reach your goals?" it is in fact also indirectly asking you, "Why do you need your MBA from *our school*?" and "How will you use *our resources* to achieve your goals?"

A common mistake among applicants when responding to this question is to simply flatter the school: "*Ross is remarkable because of its wealth of entrepreneurial resources. I am excited to join a community of aggressive and exciting innovators.*" This sentence is entirely generic; the writer has not offered any insight into his/her reasoning or into how he/she will use particular Ross resources. Instead, infuse your arguments with school-specific information. For example, this same candidate would be more effective by writing the following:

*I am interested in modernizing the antiquated wine industry but recognize that no rulebook or simple theorem exists for doing so. Thus, I am compelled by Ross's action-based learning approach, particularly its Multidisciplinary Action Project (MAP) course. During this seven-week hands-on experience on-site at a company, I expect to face "live" challenges and deliver targeted solutions, with the help of peers and advisors, meeting the high-level expectations of a major firm—the ideal training ground for facing a host of management problems in the inefficient wine industry.*

In this example, the individual does not simply compliment the school's positive qualities but explains how Ross's unique characteristics and offerings meet his/her specific needs—by inference, no other school can fulfill these needs, because no other school offers the MAP. While you may not always be able to pinpoint aspects of a program that are entirely unique to that school, the key is to show a connection between the school's resources and offerings and your individual interests and requirements—to make the

Personal Statement

association very clear and personal. Doing so will show the admissions committee that you have done your homework and understand how the full complement of that school's resources come together to create a unique and fitting experience.

As a rule of thumb, if you can answer the following three questions about the school in some detail, you will present yourself as sufficiently knowledgeable:

1. What specific/unique academic programs or classes appeal to you and will help you reach your goals?

2. How will you both contribute to and benefit from the school's non-academic offerings?

3. What elements of the school's atmosphere, the nature of its students or the general sense you get about the school through visits or conversations with students/alumni make it attractive to you?

## Two to Three Themes

In longer essays (750–1,000 words), candidates must discuss two or three key themes and give detailed explanations of exactly how they will use the school's resources to achieve their goals. For example, he/she cannot simply state: "*Columbia Business School (CBS) is an excellent choice for me because of its wealth of entrepreneurial programs. I also look forward to international programs at this most international of schools. Furthermore, CBS excels in finance and marketing.*" The idea is not to generate a list, but rather to develop a well-thought-out argument. This is similar to stating your case to a jury: prove to the admissions committee that by taking advantage of its school's specific programs in your areas of need, you will achieve your goals, and suggest that taking these specific programs is the best (or only) way for you to achieve those goals. For example, a candidate might choose to dedicate a paragraph to CBS's entrepreneurial resources:

*One of the most appealing aspects of Columbia is that entrepreneurship is not just taught but experienced through a wealth of hands-on resources. Through the Entrepreneurial Sounding Board, I will have a vital avenue available to test my ideas and gain frank feedback from serial entrepreneurs, which will allow me to refine my ideas and prevent mistakes. Equally important, I would aspire to enter the Entrepreneurial Greenhouse.*

# Personal Fit

Showing your academic and career fit with a certain program is vitally important, but so is showing your personal fit. If you have visited the school or spoken with some of its alumni, students, professors or admissions staff, mentioning these personal connections can be quite helpful. Your knowledge of the school will seem more substantial, and your interest will be seen as sincere. Note how the candidate mentions several firsthand experiences with the school in the following example:

*I was deeply impressed by my visit to the ABC School of Business. From Professor Amanda Smith's clever explanation of the AOL case in her "Acquisition Finance" course to the energy of students Tom Brown and Jill Johnson, who all but dragged me across the street to have coffee and share their insights, I was amazed at the dynamic feel that permeated my brief ABC experience. I look forward to being a part of such an outgoing community.*

# Your Contribution

Often a school will ask applicants to explain what they will bring to the greater MBA program if they are admitted as students. In this case, applicants can refer to such possible contributions as expected participation or leadership in a particular club; past work experiences, which can enrich classroom discussions; an international background, which can bring a global perspective to teams or coursework; or even personal characteristics like enthusiasm or humor, which may facilitate bonding between classmates. Be careful not just

Personal Statement

to present a list of clubs, for example, but to truly personalize your proposed involvement in specific student organizations or events and in the school's broader community. Even when a school does not explicitly ask what you can contribute, if space permits, you should still discuss what you could bring to the community, both in class and beyond, if this has not been accomplished implicitly elsewhere in the essay. Here is one example of how to address one's contributions:

*Outside the classroom, I am excited to get involved in the Operations Club, particularly the Six Sigma Challenge, given my interest in innovating within the wine industry. Needless to say, perhaps, I also look forward to joining and taking a leadership role in the Wine Tasting Club, where I could use my connections to vintners in the region to expand the club's touring program and its relationships with recruiters.*

## Why Now?

An important element of personal statement essays that sometimes gets lost in the shuffle is the "why now" aspect. Candidates understandably focus on detailing their career progress to date, outlining their goals and/or conveying why they are interested in a particular MBA program and either forget or forego any explanation of why they are choosing to pursue an MBA at this particular time. If a school specifically asks why you feel now is the right time to earn your MBA, *do not gloss over or sacrifice this information.* Do not assume that it is not as important as the other elements of your candidacy that you wish to express—the school asked about timing, and an important rule in writing any application essay is *Answer the question.* Be sure to take the time necessary to develop a clear, fitting answer to this portion of the personal statement, when asked.

# Sample Personal Statements

A) Why is an MBA a critical next step toward your short- and long-term career goals? Why is Tuck the best MBA program for you? (If you are applying for a joint or dual degree, please explain how the additional degree will contribute to those goals.) Although there is no restriction on the length of your response, most applicants use, on average, 500 words. (2009–2010 question)

*After completing my CPA designation at Ernst and Young's Philadelphia office in 2006, I transitioned from the Audit to the Mergers and Acquisitions Department, focusing on restructuring firms in bankruptcy protection. Soon after, I negotiated the sale of a $50M water-bottling company to a French conglomerate, a deal that saved 250 jobs in a one-industry town. Next, I secured $80M for a metal recycling firm, just in time for the commodities boom. Because of such transactions, I found my work intellectually challenging and personally meaningful.[1] Still, I want to achieve more—I want to secure the enduring survival of troubled firms.*

*My long-term career goal is therefore to acquire a distressed firm and lead its turnaround by reshaping its operations and strategy. After identifying an ailing industry, I plan to purchase a struggling firm, leverage this acquisition's success and consolidate additional firms, ultimately realizing "deep value" for investors, employees and society.[2] To achieve this, after graduating from Tuck, I intend to join either the Performance Improvement Group at Bain and Company, specializing in turnaround strategy, or the Operations Group at BCG, focusing on Rigorous Program Improvement.[3] With three to five years of consulting experience recommend-*

---

1   If you read the question carefully, you will see that it is not asking you to recount your development over the past several years (unlike the question in Sample Personal Statement B). Therefore, you do not need to discuss your progress since college. You just need to provide brief context.

2   The candidate is not required to follow a structure of short-term goals followed by long-term goals, so he chooses to immediately lay out ambitious long-term goals that are directly connected to his previous work with distressed firms. He then follows with his short-term goals.

3   The candidate is not simply saying, "I want to be a generic consultant." He displays considerable focus and a clear understanding of both where he would fit at these firms and how these positions connect with his stated goals.

*ing strategic and operational changes for a multitude of "challenged" firms, I would be ideally prepared to identify my own niche turnaround opportunity.*

*Gaining my CPA gave me specialized financial knowledge, but to achieve my goal I need theoretical and practical exposure to all management disciplines. Tuck stands out for me among MBA programs because its sole academic focus is the MBA, and the core of its program is general management. Tuck's core curriculum is especially compelling, not only because of its breadth, but also because of its immediate focus on management decision making via the "Analysis for General Managers" mini-course and the "Leading Organizations" and "Competitive Corporate Strategy" courses. Moreover, Tuck's practical opportunities uniquely reinforce principles of strategic thinking. Speaking with current student John Doe, I was excited to discover I could work with like-minded professors and peers to shape both my First Year Project and the Tuck Global Consultancy experience around my turnaround learning objectives. Through these remarkable hands-on projects, I could develop my own targeted learning principles in a "live" environment and on the global stage. Furthermore, I would immerse myself in the Cohen Leadership Program to benefit from the consistent feedback of peers, mentors and coaches, with respect to refining my management style.[1]*

*When I visited Tuck this fall, Tuck Connections matched me with fellow CPA Jane Doe, who guided me on a campus tour and then invited me to join her study group. I had heard about Tuck's culture, but that evening I experienced it firsthand by joining a vibrant discussion on "The Boeing Problem" and being challenged by the diversity of opinions represented. I was hooked. Tuck's MBA program—the study groups, small class size, sole focus on the MBA and the warmth and dynamism of the commu-*

Personal Statement

---

1 The detail in this section clearly indicates that this candidate has done his homework. He delves into the structure of the curriculum, discusses the appeal of the required core and names several Tuck-specific programs in relation to his stated goals. The reader would not doubt his interest.

*nity—provides a unique learning atmosphere that will propel me into my ambitious career.[2]*

B) Describe your career progress to date and your future short-term and long-term career goals. How do you expect a Wharton MBA to help you achieve these goals, and why is now the best time for you to join our program? (1,000 words; 2008–2009 question)

*Declining an offer from a Wall Street investment bank after graduating with a degree in Economics from Chicago, I chose a path that stunned my friends and even my family. I returned to San Antonio to join Gimli Furniture—my family's firm. While I admired my father's success in growing this high-end retail business from a single-location store into an eight-location chain, we both acknowledged that the firm needed to be reinvented. I therefore joined as Marketing Manager to reinvigorate our Marketing Department, which I quickly realized was stuck in the past. In my first three months, I overhauled our Web site and simultaneously launched e-coupons—a heresy in the high-end furniture world. We soon saw a surge in online and in-store traffic, as well as a sustained 15% increase in monthly sales.[3]*

*Building on this success, I approached my father with another unorthodox idea, but one that met our goal of reinvention—expanding outside Texas. He was initially hesitant, because he knew the local market well. He grasped the potential, however, once I developed a formal business plan that identified nearby Arizona as an ideal expansion destination, given the high number of affluent retirees—our primary customer base—who settle there annually.*

Personal Statement

---

2  By revealing a priori experience with the school, the candidate emphasizes his interest and his fit with its MBA program. It is important that you show not only that you will gain the professional training you need while at the school, but also that you will thrive in the community.

3  When discussing a family business, it is important for candidates to show that they have made the most of the opportunity and have had an impact of their own on the organization.

*As I embarked on an adventure to open our new Arizona store, I did not have access to our Texas infrastructure and was essentially operating as a small business person. Whether I was hiring almost 100 staff members, developing a public relations campaign, managing negotiations with the bank for inventory financing or creating a supply chain from scratch, I was exhilarated by the lead-up to our opening. I felt an incredible sense of pride when my father and I cut the ribbon on our Scottsdale store on Labor Day 2005. Since then, Gimli-Arizona has exceeded expectations, and within two years, we opened two more stores; now these three are our highest grossing (by our metric of revenue per square feet). My father and I clearly see that Gimli once again has a bold future ahead.*

*Last Thanksgiving, I returned home to San Antonio, and before I even had a bite of turkey, my father started a conversation that would change my life. He told me he was thrilled with our success and wanted me to expand Gimli across the Southwest, before he turned the business over to me in a few years—five at most. He had sketched the terms out in a notebook and stated that, in time, he would begin a well-earned retirement and I would become the company's president.[1] After collecting myself, I set only one condition—that I first earn an MBA. I quoted my father to himself: "Whatever you do, do it right." For me, "doing Gimli Furniture right" means earning my MBA—from Wharton. Only with a Wharton MBA, given the school's strengths in entrepreneurship, finance and family business management, will I possess the skills I need to expand Gimli into a regional chain in the short term and into a national chain thereafter.[2]*

*In my case, studying entrepreneurship will be essential as I continue to transform our organization. At Wharton, I would pursue the Entrepreneurial Management major. Through courses such as "Strategies and Practices of Family-Controlled Companies" and "Legal Issues Facing En-*

---

1 The candidate does not simply recite the basic information from his resume, but instead creates a narrative that reveals what is unique about this his experiences. Remember, you are telling a story about yourself!
2 The writer clearly states why he is pursuing an MBA.

trepreneurs," I will lay the foundation for expanding Gimli nationally. Further, "Building Human Assets in Entrepreneurial Ventures" will enable me to tackle an ongoing challenge we face—attracting and retaining excellent people despite our limited financial resources. Through the Entrepreneur in Residence Program, I will receive feedback from experienced mentors and continue to reconsider Gimli's long-held but possibly antiquated operating principles. Finally, via the Wharton Business Plan Competition, I could test a new concept-store targeted at a younger demographic, and could thereby both learn about possibilities for my firm and test my entrepreneurial mettle.[3]

While I do not intend to proceed into a classic finance-related career, finance will still be important to my education, because Gimli's expansion will depend on large, complex financial arrangements. Thus, "Real Estate Investments" will enable me to determine whether Gimli should expand into rented or owned facilities, and "Corporate Valuation" and "The Finance of Buyouts and Acquisitions" will prepare me to seize long-term growth opportunities. I appreciate the rich array of finance resources offered via the White Center and am particularly excited that the traditional focus of its annual seminar is on household financial decision making, since almost all Gimli's furniture is purchased for the home.[4]

Beyond Wharton's broad course offerings, I am also drawn to the school because of the remarkable expertise it has developed with respect to the unique challenges faced by family businesses. Not only would I benefit from family business–oriented courses and from student groups such as the Wharton Family Business Club, I would immerse myself in family business research at the Wharton Global Family Alliance (WGFA). Wharton's foresight in recognizing the important role family firms play in

Personal Statement

---

3  Because the word limit for this essay is larger than that for Sample Personal Statement A, this candidate is able to go into tremendous depth about why Wharton is the right choice for him. Here he explains in detail how the school's entrepreneurial offerings will facilitate his goals.

4  Again, with the greater allowed word count, the candidate can go into great detail—in this case, explaining his need for certain financial skills and naming the specific resources at Wharton that fulfill that need.

*today's business world—and its leadership in establishing the WGFA—immediately made me feel that the Wharton MBA program is uniquely suited to my needs.[1]*

*Ultimately, however, what draws me to Wharton is the vibrancy and diversity of its community—something I saw for myself when I visited last month. Sitting in on "Statistical Modeling" with Professor Robert Stine was incredible; the sparkle and humor in the classroom discussion turned complex numbers into a simple but profound forecasting lesson. My student guide, Jane Doe, took me on a campus tour, and I could not get over how she enthused about Wharton—as did, quite literally, the dozens of people I spoke to with Jane. The students I met in Huntsman Hall were friendly and energetic, but most of all passionate about their studies, their future and their Wharton experience. That is what I want out of an MBA program. I want to be equally passionate about my studies, my future career at Gimli Furniture and my overall MBA experience—and Wharton, more than anywhere else, will bring out that passion.[2]*

C) a. Briefly describe your short-term and long-term career goals.

b. Why is an MBA the best choice at this point in your career?

c. What and/or who influenced your decision to apply to Ross? (500–word maximum total; 2009–2010 question)

*"Talk to your daughter before the beauty industry does," warned an attention-grabbing Dove advertisement. When Dove launched its Campaign for Real Beauty, I witnessed its impact firsthand, as it ignited passionate conversations on body-image issues among my friends. After four years developing film trailers, posters and merchandise for feature*

---

1 In this paragraph, the candidate enumerates Wharton's unique programs related to family business, again showing that he has fully researched the school and that his interest is serious!

2 By sharing the story of his campus visit and his interactions with members of the Wharton community, the candidate demonstrates here that he is not only an academic fit with the school but also a personality fit.

*releases as an associate at Bohemia, a boutique entertainment marketing firm, I felt the need to pursue a path that would allow me to have a greater and more meaningful influence on others.*

*Seeking to remain in marketing, I began to pursue informational interviews, eventually landing one with a product director at Dove. I was amazed at the detailed information Dove had collected through its interactive media campaigns, as it strived to reach millions of "daughters" first.[3] I am now inspired to join a socially conscious firm as a brand manager to help solve the puzzle that is the consumer while simultaneously promoting a healthy lifestyle. In this role, I would be steadily promoted and ultimately manage multiple brands, learning about unique marketing challenges and the rapidly evolving, data-driven market at each step.[4] Ultimately, I plan to start my own marketing consulting firm, using my corporate experience and MBA training to help small socially aware firms carve out their niches. At Bohemia, I have seen small films emerge as blockbusters—as an entrepreneur, I will help companies create blockbuster consumer products.[5]*

*Ross's general management approach appeals to me because I know that marketing is often complexly intertwined with operations and finance. Professor Christie Nordheilm's "Big Picture" marketing course will teach me key frameworks to structure my approach to developing strategies and communications plans for both new and established consumer products. In Professor Terry Duncan's "Leveraging Marketing in Industrial Design" class, I will learn to unify consumer data and influence design, tailoring products to consumer needs. When I visited Ross in October 2009, I attended the Marketing Symposium and was impressed with*

3 For this essay, a comprehensive work history is neither requested nor appropriate, so the writer provides just enough background information to serve as context for the "Why an MBA?" and "What influenced your decision?" portions of her response.

4 Here the specificity of the candidate's goal shows that she has direction and focus—she is not just seeking a marketing position, she is targeting a brand manager role in a socially conscious firm that promotes a healthy lifestyle.

5 The candidate's long term-goals are ambitious, yet realistic.

Personal Statement

*the student participants' depth of knowledge and the content of the panel discussions—from social marketing to design to advertising and branding. At Ross, I could clearly "live" marketing both inside and outside the classroom.[1]*

*On campus, I also met Edward Thompson, president of Net Impact, and am excited about the strength of this chapter. Joining this group and participating in its annual symposium and Social Intraprenuers Alumni Panel would certainly be professionally valuable, but just a side benefit of contributing to this important organization and establishing enduring friendships with classmates. In addition to joining the Marketing and Entertainment and Media clubs, which intellectually interest me, I plan to contribute my creative talents to videos and skits for Rock 'n' Roll B-School and Ross Follies. I have seen firsthand that Ross has an engaged community of students, professors and administration, and I know I truly fit this environment. I hope to assume leadership roles and make an impact at the school, just as I intend to make an impact in my career, benefiting companies and consumers alike.[2]*

D) How did you choose your most recent job/internship and how did this experience influence your future goals? What about the Chicago Booth MBA makes you feel it is the next best step in your career at this time? (750–1,000 words; 2009–2010 question)

*In a gripping 15-minute meeting, armed with just five PowerPoint slides, I informed my managing director that he was emphasizing the wrong things in our new organization and needed to start focusing on people. I suggested he hire me as an HR strategy manager to help fix this problem. In this role, I would coordinate training initiatives firm-wide,*

---

1 By making note of specific resources at the school and relating them to her stated goals, the candidate helps establish her credibility with the reader.

2 In this paragraph, the writer reinforces what Ross offers in her spheres of interest—marketing and socially oriented business—while also revealing her personal fit with the school and a desire to contribute to the Ross community.

*develop process improvements to reduce non-value-added work and help management address other urgent strategic HR challenges.[3]*

*After my boss had agreed to my new role and the modest raise I had also requested, I took a breath and considered what I had accomplished. I had been managing Jedang's expatriate hiring program and English language training initiatives in Bangkok and had already hired ten employees who were flourishing within the company when, unexpectedly, Adroitte Consulting suddenly acquired the firm. With the advent of new international standards, management rushed to bring everyone up to speed on the new regulations and client service guidelines. Added demands and pressure from the top were taking a toll on my already overworked Thai colleagues, and I could no longer just sit by and watch. Only after the meeting did I realize how much courage it had taken to confront my boss; luckily, he had graciously welcomed my feedback.*

*During the next six months, I was immersed in the five-year strategic planning process for the entire organization. For two weeks in particular, the managing directors of the five service divisions and I burned the midnight oil, crafting the firm's major goals and a corporate growth framework. Given my Thai and English language abilities, I managed the creation of the firm's Five-Year Strategic Action Plan. My personal passion for employee growth and development led me to emphasize employee satisfaction as a key metric of the plan's success, and I outlined milestones and actions to reach that goal.*

*To persuade the team to include HR goals in the strategic plan, I used analyses of employee satisfaction numbers, something my mentor, David Nguyen,[4] a 1978 Chicago Booth alumnus and now CEO of the*

---

3  The candidate uses an engaging narrative opening to capture the reader's interest, rather than simply presenting bullets from her resume about her most recent promotion.

4  Here the candidate shows an important personal connection to the school. The "name dropping" in this context is not forced or for show—this person has played a significant role in the candidate's professional success and also in her interest in Chicago Booth in particular.

*new Adroitte Thailand, encouraged me to do. On the surface, employee satisfaction numbers were weak and declining, but the rate of change— the second derivative of employee satisfaction—painted an even bleaker picture. Overall approval had fallen an alarming 10% in the previous six months, versus 6% in the previous three years combined. The second derivative always tells the truth, David had taught me. Using this data, I convinced the strategic action plan committee to eliminate mandatory Saturday workdays, hold monthly town hall meetings and implement process improvements to reduce overwork—productivity and employee happiness quickly began to rise.*

*Profoundly influencing the decisions of an enormous multinational corporation was very inspiring. I want to reach other organizations in this way and use my belief in employee empowerment and fulfillment to transform how companies engage with their employees. To extend my reach and maximize my effectiveness, I will need an MBA.*

*I ultimately see myself moving into HR consulting and will likely join an HR consulting firm after graduation to gain more hands-on experience in managing change in large organizations. However, I may first work as a strategy management consultant to deepen my understanding of the range of strategic business issues and their resolution before specializing in HR consulting. As an HR consultant, I will help companies restructure their organizations to ensure that employees have fulfilling career paths and appropriate work-life balance.[1]*

*In talking with David about Chicago Booth, I came to see how the school's rigorous academic environment, culture of challenging the obvious and emphasis on advanced economics as the foundation for all good business decisions shaped his view of industry and his place in it. He credits the program with providing the tools and network he needed to*

---

1  The school's question is rather vague with respect to the candidate's ambitions—asking generally about "future goals" but not specifically for short- or long-term plans. So, the candidate justifiably does not offer detailed intentions but still shows purpose and thoughtfulness in moving in a particular direction in her career.

*build his career. To realize my goals in the HR arena, I aim to follow in his footsteps.*

*Beyond the important foundational courses "Microeconomics"—which I hope to take with Kevin Murphy to give my initial economic insight training an extra boost—"Corporate Finance" and "Managerial Decision-Making," the classes "Managing in Organizations" and "Strategic Management" seem uniquely tailored to my needs. They will teach me to explore frameworks for organizational design and people management, thus equipping me to advise future clients in these areas. And after gaining a solid foundation in management essentials—accounting, economics, corporate finance, statistics—I will concentrate in organizational behavior to explore people-organization relationships in depth.*

*Chicago Booth is also ideal for my needs because of the ample opportunities available to start implementing the lessons of the MBA classroom in the field through the student groups that engage local businesses in an advisory capacity. Via the Business Solutions Group in particular, I hope to consult to a small Chicago business or nonprofit to gain insight into the hands-on challenges of real client management as well as the myriad facets of a business that determine and are affected by strategic HR management. Such opportunities will not only cement classroom learnings, but also provide me with the softer, more ephemeral skills that can truly only be gained hands-on.*

*I am especially looking forward to participating in the greater Chicago Booth community. While visiting the school, I spoke with second year Amy Smart, who told me about the many opportunities to bond with fellow classmates and form lasting relationships through team-building and social activities, such as the LEAD program and weekly Happy Hour. I know the connections I will form with my LEAD teammates will extend well into my career. Also, with my extensive background in theater and film production, I hope to participate in and help produce Follies, enjoy-*

Personal Statement

155

*ing with my classmates the shared creative process that a stage production uniquely offers.[1]*

*With a Chicago Booth MBA, I will clearly be well positioned to succeed in a career in strategic HR management and consulting. The challenge, rigor and growth I will experience both inside and outside the classroom will enable me to more significantly influence organizations and the way they manage their employees.*

# A Special Focus on Career Changers

As we noted earlier in this chapter, many business school applicants are interested in earning their MBA as a way of changing careers. Although schools recognize this trend, they also have to satisfy the needs of their recruiters, most of whom come to campus to hire applicants who already have depth of experience in their field—even more so during difficult economic times, when they tend to become increasingly conservative in their hiring practices. Even when hiring is robust, however, career changers in particular need to be able to prove that they "fit" with their new target career. To effectively do so, they must highlight the components of their past that have provided them with applicable foundational experience or transferable skills for their future career. To help with this, we have created a worksheet, whose purpose is to help you

- determine the skills and past experiences you should emphasize in your personal statement that will demonstrate continuity, themes and transferable skills.

- think through your short-term goals.

---

1 Here the candidate demonstrates indisputably that she "knows" Chicago Booth and has made a personal connection with the school. If you were to remove the Chicago Booth name, the essay would no longer make sense—thus proving that the essay is not generic but specific to this one school alone.

- distill your personal statement down to a one-page snapshot, which you will use as a guide.

A completed sample worksheet, as well as a blank one, appears at the end of this chapter for use in helping you narrow in on your goals. To complete the worksheet, follow these eight steps:

1. Enter a summary statement of your long-term goal in Box A, labeled "Long-Term Goal." The reason for starting at the end in this way is to help you focus on your ultimate vision of where you want to be with your career; this will in turn help you decide which skills or traits you will need to be able to attain that goal (and which you will need to emphasize in your essay).

2. In Box B, the "Skills/Traits" box directly underneath the "Long-Term Goal" box, list eight to ten skills or traits you will need to be successful in pursuing your long-term goal. These can include skills/traits you already have as well as ones you do not yet possess. Think about "hard" skills, like financial analysis or expertise in writing business plans, as well as "soft" skills, like the ability to motivate or inspire others. The purpose of this box is for you to think creatively and comprehensively about what competencies you need to achieve your goal. By then looking at which competencies you already have achieved and which ones you still need (as you will do in completing the following steps), you will clarify what you will need to emphasize in your personal statement.

3. In Box C, the "Skills/Traits" box directly underneath Box D, "Experience," list which of the skills/traits you identified in Step 2 you already possess (i.e., that you have gained from your professional, community or personal experiences). Note: this list should be shorter than the list in Step 2, because *in this case, you are listing only those skills/traits that you already possess.* The goal of this step is to determine which of your current competencies are

important for your long-term goal; these are the traits you will emphasize in your personal statement. For example, let's say that one such trait is an ability to motivate a team, and you do not have any work-related team leadership experience. However, you were captain of a championship basketball team in college. You might not originally have thought of mentioning that college experience, but by listing in Step 2 all the traits you need for your long-term goal, you now know that this team leadership experience is in fact relevant.

4. In Box D, labeled "Experience," enter a summary statement of the specific experiences that relate to the skills/traits you just listed in Step 3. Using our example from Step 3, in this box, you would list your experience as captain of the championship-winning college basketball team.

5. In Box E, the "Skills/Traits" box located directly underneath Box F, "MBA," list which skills/traits you expect to gain from earning your MBA degree. Note that this list will be shorter than the list in Step 2, because *in this case, you are detailing only those skills/traits you still need to gain.* The purpose of this list is to help you identify aspects of the school—specific classes, clubs, excursions, other resources—that will help prepare you to pursue your goals.

6. In Box F, the "MBA" box, summarize the list you just created in Step 5 into a description of what you want to gain from your MBA experience.

7. Look now at the list of skills/traits that you listed in Box B (Step 2) and cross off any that you have listed in Step 3 (those you already possess) or Step 5 (those you will gain in business school). Which skills/traits are left? Those missing skills/traits are what you need your short-term goal to provide. List these in Box G,

labeled "Skills/Traits," directly underneath Box H, "Short-Term Goal."

8. In Box H, labeled "Short-Term Goal," write a summary statement of your short-term goal. Ideally, your short-term goal will provide you with the skills/traits listed in Box G (Step 7).

When you have completed these steps, what you will have is a one-page snapshot of your personal statement. This worksheet will help you avoid simply repeating elements from your resume or using up your allotted word count relating experiences that are not connected to your goals. It will help you tell a story that has continuity and that clearly emphasizes which skills you already have and which you still need to obtain. Although you most likely will not—and probably should not—write the essay linearly (as the information now appears on your worksheet), being able to see all the key components of the essay in one place is extremely helpful and helps ensure that you have addressed all the necessary points.

# Sample Completed Worksheet

**This worksheet will help you accomplish the following:**

1) Determine the skills and past experiences you should emphasize in your personal statement that will demonstrate continuity, themes and transferable skills.

2) Think through your short-term goals.

3) Distill your personal statement down to a one-page snapshot, which you will use as a guide.

| D. Experience | F. MBA | H. Short-Term Goal | A. Long-Term Goal |
|---|---|---|---|
| Operations major, worked for three years in China, spent childhood in developing country | Must focus on finance, HR, consulting and build skills in these areas; join clubs for hands-on experience | Obtain position consulting in a developing country | To consult with factories in developing countries on operational improvements |
| **C. Skills/Traits:** | **E. Skills/Traits:** | **G. Skills/Traits:** | **B. Skills/Traits:** |
| • English, Chinese<br>• Operations experience in China<br>• Empathy/no judgment (childhood perspective)<br>• Leading team at work; developed motivation skills | • Volunteer, Consulting Club = first-hand knowledge<br>• Finance skills—Finance Club<br>• Alumni network<br>• Take electives on HR challenges in other countries | • Work for Bain/BCG in China, Ops division<br>• Find mentor I can learn motivation skills from<br>• Improve operational knowledge | • Consulting and teaching skills<br>• Languages (English, Chinese, Indonesian)<br>• Finance skills<br>• Motivational techniques<br>• Ability to suspend judgment, empathy<br>•HR tools & knowledge<br>• Operations experience |

# Blank Worksheet

**This worksheet will help you accomplish the following:**

1) Determine the skills and past experiences you should emphasize in your personal statement that will demonstrate continuity, themes and transferable skills.

2) Think through your short-term goals.

3) Distill your personal statement down to a one-page snapshot, which you will use as a guide.

| D. Experience | F. MBA | H. Short-Term Goal | A. Long-Term Goal |
|---|---|---|---|
|  |  |  |  |

| C. Skills/Traits: | E. Skills/Traits: | G. Skills/Traits: | B. Skills/Traits: |
|---|---|---|---|
|  |  |  |  |

**Box A:** Enter a summary statement of your long-term goal.

**Box B:** List eight to ten skills/traits you will need to be successful in attaining your long-term goal.

**Box C:** List which of the skills/traits in Box B you have already gained from your professional, community or personal experiences.

**Box D:** Enter a summary statement of the specific experiences that relate to the skills/traits in Box C.

**Box E:** List the skills/traits you expect to gain from earning your MBA degree.

**Box F:** Summarize the list from Box E into a description of what you want from your MBA experience.

**Box G:** List the skills from Box B that have not been listed in Boxes C or E.

**Box H:** Enter a summary statement of your short-term goal.

# Letters of Recommendation

Chapter 6

# *Part I: For Candidates*

We at mbaMission believe that, for both strategic and ethical reasons, your recommenders—not you—should write your letters of recommendation. Writing an objective, self-aware letter highlighting your own strengths can be very difficult. Also challenging is revealing aspects of your personality that have not yet been highlighted in your essays. We encourage you, therefore, to seek recommenders who will write a recommendation for you themselves rather than asking you to write it. To best illustrate the guidelines we present here for both candidates and recommenders, we provide a sample of the notes applicants can provide to their recommender(s) and a resulting recommendation later in this chapter.

## Choosing Your Recommenders

Who can write a valuable letter? Like many candidates, you may believe that your recommenders must have remarkable credentials and titles to impress the admissions committee. However, what is far more important is selecting individuals who can write a personal and intimate letter that discusses your talents, accomplishments, personality and potential. If senior managers at your company can only describe your work in vague and general terms, they will not help your cause. By contrast, lower-level managers who directly supervise your work can often offer powerful examples of the impact you have on your company, and their letters can be far more effective at getting you accepted into an MBA program.

Nonetheless, not all people who know you and your capabilities intimately will make good recommenders. For starters, of course, you should have some confidence that the potential recommender likes you and will write a positive letter on your behalf! As you contemplate your choices, try to gather some intelligence on your potential recommenders. Have they written letters for anyone else? Are they generous with their time with regard to employee feedback and review sessions? Will they devote the effort and time necessary to write a letter that will really shine?

One of the best ways to anticipate your chances for success with certain potential recommenders is to learn how things worked for former colleagues who have also needed letters of recommendation for MBA programs. If possible, speak with them to discover how your supervisor managed the process. By identifying those who will be helpful and generous in providing a recommendation, you will alleviate the possible stresses of missed deadlines and unpredictable or unhelpful letters.

If your prospective MBA program asks for two letters of recommendation, then generally, you should approach two of your recent supervisors. Ideally, one should be your current supervisor. Your letters will have added credibility if they are written by individuals who are senior to you, because your recommenders are in evaluative positions and will not have anything to lose by critically appraising your candidacy.

If you are not in a position to ask your current superiors for a recommendation, you should explain this with a few very brief sentences in your optional essay—do not worry, this is a common problem. In fact, we estimate that one of every five applicants has an issue with one of their current supervisors which prevents them from asking for a recommendation. Common issues include the following:

- Brief tenure with current firm

- Disclosing business school plans could compromise promotions, bonuses or potential increases in salary

- Supervisor is "too busy" to help and either refuses the request or tells the applicant to write the recommendation him/herself, which the applicant is unprepared to do (and which is not advised)

- Supervisor does not believe in the MBA degree and would not be supportive of this path

- Supervisor is a poor manager and refuses to assist junior staff

- Candidate is an entrepreneur or works in a family business and thus lacks a credible supervisor

Common sense dictates that the admissions office has no reason to disadvantage one group (those who have issues with recommenders) over another (those who have secured recommendations from supervisors). What incentive would schools have to "disqualify" approximately 20% of the applicant pool for reasons beyond the candidates' control?

So, if you cannot ask your supervisor for his/her assistance, you should not be too concerned about your situation but should of course seek to remedy it. Start by considering alternatives, such as a mentor, past employer, supplier, client, legal counsel, representative from an industry association or anyone else who knows your work particularly well. Then, once you have made your alternate selection, you should use the optional essay to briefly explain the nature of your situation and your relationship with this recommender. As long as you explain your choice, the admissions committee will understand and appreciate your situation.

# Managing the Process

Take the time to meet with your selected recommenders before they write your recommendations. This is vitally important, and most candidates do not think to take this important step. You can even remind your recommenders about stories involving them that could be usefully recounted in the letters they will write.

Reviewing your accomplishments and contributions with your recommenders is perfectly ethical. In fact, Stanford's Assistant Dean and Director of MBA Admissions Derek Bolton encourages you to do so. In a letter to prospective students, Bolton stated:

> *"You then have occasion to have several candid conversations about your personal and professional development with these individuals who are committed to your success. Through these discussions, you can get feedback that will help you better understand your own strengths and development needs, make a larger impact in your current position, build stronger working relationships, and refine your personal and professional aspirations. In other words, instead of viewing this process as a means to an end (the letter of recommendation), I encourage you to view this process as a valuable experience in and of itself. If you do so, I believe your recommender will produce a more powerful letter of recommendation because the process itself will have been so compelling. Further, you will learn more this way!"*

[Read the full letter at www.gsb.stanford.edu/mba/admission/dir_references-p.html]

During such a session with a recommender, you should refresh his/her memories with respect to your accomplishments and progress. Make clear your reasons for pursuing your MBA, your reasons for choosing the schools you are targeting and your ambitions post-graduation. Give your recommenders your resume and, ideally, a separate list of accomplishments that occurred directly under their supervision (*see the example list provided at the end of this chapter*) so they can easily include key examples of your accomplishments and potential in their letters. Most importantly, impress upon your recommenders the importance of providing real-life evidence wherever possible. (We know from working with some overseas clients that robust, example-filled letters of recommendation are unusual in many countries—if this is the case in your country, do your best to explain to your recommender the importance of full answers laden with examples.)

Your recommenders will not be judged on their eloquence but rather on their insights. As long as your recommendation letter is personal, sincere and thorough, your recommenders have done their job. Indeed, recommenders need not even speak or write English terribly well—all that matters is that their ideas are understandable and compelling.

Depending on your relationship with your recommenders, you may want to share with them the guidelines we provide for recommenders on the following pages.

# Thinking Ahead

If you are starting this process early, you can take an important step and get in touch with former supervisors with whom you have fallen out of contact. You do not want to be in a position where you are calling a former supervisor for the first time in years and asking him/her for a big favor on a tight timeline. If you can identify a former supervisor whose help you will solicit, make contact now, and then keep the relationship warm over the next few months. You will be far better off when the letter-writing process begins.

You should consider giving your recommenders extra-early "personal" submission deadlines. By doing so, you will ensure that your recommenders complete their letters ahead of the MBA program's schedule (and thus on time). Then, if your recommenders miss your personal deadline, you will still be in good shape, because you will have built in extra time for them to complete the letter before the school's hard, official deadline.

If you are applying to more than one school, remember that this may mean your recommenders will have to rework the same letter—or even answer different questions about you—as required by your various applications. You will do yourself a huge service if, when you initially approach your recommenders, you tell them up front that you would like for them to provide a letter of recommendation for each of the schools to which you will apply (i.e., that they will need to prepare more than one such letter, perhaps in more than one format). That way, when you begin work on additional applications, you won't have to go back to your recommender and say, "Oh, by the way, would you mind doing another letter now?"

# Part II: For Recommenders

Recommendation letters are a vital aspect of a business school applicant's profile because they offer the admissions committees their only truly objective window into the candidate's abilities. For this reason, recommenders can contribute significantly to a candidate's chances for success, but only if their letters are written in a credible and compelling manner.

## Maximizing Your Impact

To ensure that your letter will maximize the candidate's chances of being admitted to business school, you must provide full, descriptive answers filled with actual examples of the candidate's accomplishments and potential—this is essential. To that end, we highly recommend that you meet with the candidate to discuss his/her accomplishments (not his/her *responsibilities*, but what he/she has actually *achieved* and/or brought to pass!). Strive to understand why the candidate was effective and what he/she could have improved in each project or task. Nothing is ethically wrong with meeting with the candidate and discussing these matters—in fact, several top MBA schools encourage such meetings, which can help you formulate a clearer picture of the applicant.

During your meeting with the candidate, do your best to really understand his/her ambitions, reasons for seeking an MBA and rationale for choosing a particular school. Again, the more you know about your candidate and the more you understand his/her approach, the more you will be able to bolster that person's candidacy.

As you write, consider each question an opportunity for you to influence the MBA admissions committee. However, this does not mean that you should discuss the candidate ad nauseam—carefully observe any word limits. Short, powerful statements that reference real-life examples are more valuable than long, wordy answers that are vague or unfocused. At the same time, try to avoid writing only the minimum. For example, your Letter of Recommendation form may request the following:

> **Please describe your relationship with the candidate, citing how long you have known the candidate and the length of time that you have supervised him/her.**
>
> Answer: *"I am the Director of Marketing at XYZ Corp., and I have been Jodi's boss for approximately three years."*

This answer does almost nothing to positively support the candidate. It is strictly factual and does not offer any real endorsement or differentiating value. In the following example, however, the recommender seizes the opportunity to establish his/her own credibility as well as offer details on the candidate's successes.

> **Please describe your relationship with the candidate, citing how long you have known the candidate and the length of time that you have supervised him/her.**
>
> Answer: *"I am the Director of Marketing for XYZ Corp., but I first met Jodi three years ago, when I was VP of Product Sales. At that time, I personally hired Jodi as the first member of our New York sales team, and since then, I have seen her professional skills rapidly develop. At first, Jodi leveraged her personality and work ethic to become a leading salesperson*

*nationwide. She truly blossomed as a manager after her promotion to New York Sales Coordinator and then to VP East Coast Sales. As I have advanced at XYZ, Jodi has done so in lockstep, so I have witnessed these stages of her career firsthand and therefore feel well qualified to comment on her experiences and potential."*

As you write, also consider that your letter is not an opportunity to "sell" the candidate to the admissions committee. You should let the candidate's actions speak for themselves and use facts to substantiate your claims. Real-life examples add credibility to your statements and to your ability to comment on the candidate's achievements.

Superlatives and generalities like *"Tom is the most wonderful employee in the world and a great guy!"* are actually not helpful, primarily because they are too vague to be useful in making the candidate stand out among other applicants. However, superlatives that are paired with context and "proof" (via examples/experiences) can add tremendous value:

*"Tom's analytical skills are second to none. As a Research Associate, Tom prepared an insightful and original research note on inflation in Peru that caught the attention of our Research Director. Soon, as a second-year employee, Tom was de facto promoted to work among a group of our Senior Economists, many of whom had more than a decade of experience."*

Simply stating that Tom's skills are second to none would not have been enough, but offering hard evidence for this claim immediately thereafter ("insightful and original research," "de facto promotion") reinforces this declaration and makes the argument convincing. **This is not selling—this is persuasion.** In general, offering two or three attributes with clear and detailed examples to illustrate them is probably sufficient.

The concept of differentiation is quite important, because MBA programs want to know they will be accepting an elite applicant, not an average employee. Thus, any comparison to the candidate's peers is welcome, but the comparison should put the candidate at the top, and this placement should be substantiated by evidence. (More guidance on numerical or quantitative ranking of a candidate is provided later in this chapter.)

### What are the candidate's strengths and weaknesses?

*"Bill stands out among his peers because of his extraordinary communication and interpersonal skills. He has used his confidence, sharp wit and sense of humor to capture audiences' imagination and has been the only one of our six VPs to be requested as a guest speaker at another region's annual sales conference (and has since been asked back twice). Bill is also quite engaging and charismatic on a one-on-one level and has used his personality to motivate others and create one of our highest-performing teams, earning him two promotions ahead of his peers."*

In this case, the reader is told that Bill has some extraordinary skills, and this claim is supported by the revelations that (1) he has been the **only** one invited to a certain event, (2) that he **created one of the company's highest performing teams** and (3) and that he was promoted **ahead of his peers**—three differentiating facts that reveal the candidate to be elite.

## Honest Evaluation

Critical feedback—not *negative*, but critical—adds credibility to your recommendations. You may be reluctant to write anything critical, but as long as your comments are constructive (and limited), you will add value to your recommendations. However, you should not present a "disguised strength" as a weakness—a peeve of admissions officials:

*"Suzanne often works too hard. I have pushed her to take more breaks and vacations, but she is just too dedicated."*

The sentence is disingenuous, and the admissions committee will detect this and immediately discount the answer—and possibly your entire letter.

Still, "too much" honesty is likewise unhelpful. Writing "*Suzanne is horribly lazy*," for example, would be quite detrimental. If you sincerely feel that your comments about a candidate would be primarily negative or unhelpful to him/her in gaining admission to an MBA program, you should advise the candidate to look elsewhere for a recommendation.

Ideally, you should strike a balance between being honest and not being hurtful:

> "*Suzanne is strong as a motivator and can always rouse our team. Still, I think she needs one more 'arrow in her quiver.' I would like to see her exhibit more sensitivity to our employees' needs in one-on-one situations.*"

## Examples, Not Word Count

No specific length is ideal for a recommendation letter (unless, of course, the admissions committee has requested a set limit); your responses just need to be thorough, thoughtful and laden with examples. Often, "less is more." If you try to highlight a dozen strengths for a candidate, you will most likely dilute all the strengths presented, thereby rendering none of them particularly effective. On the other hand, if you highlight just three strengths and convincingly cite examples to illustrate them, you will have done your job. The average MBA recommendation might be two or three pages long, but this varies. Substance and depth are more important than length.

## Rankings

Some schools will issue recommendation forms that ask you to rank the candidate within a specific percentage range for certain characteristics or skills, such as "Compared to employees of a similar level, would you say that the candidate is in the top 2% of his/her peers, the top 25% of his/her peers, etc.?" In such cases, the candidate would be best served being ranked highly, of course, yet also fairly and honestly. Simply ranking the candidate among the top percentage across the board will likely not be believable to the admissions committee and could ultimately be less helpful than intended. Your candidate should be ranked among the top in the areas in which they are truly strongest, but for credibility reasons, he/she should be ranked less high—though still well—in areas where he/she is not quite as accomplished. If you feel that you cannot credibly do this, you may want to speak with the candidate about this before writing your letter, because this may affect the candidate's chances of being accepted.

You will find a sample list of accomplishments (which the candidate would provide to his/her recommender) and sample responses (what the recommender would submit to the school) on the following pages.

# *Sample List of Accomplishments for MBA Recommendation Review Session*

**Steve Smith, MBA Candidate**

**John Brown, President, ABC Metal Co. (ABCM)**

**<u>Background</u>:**

- First employee hired via ABCM's on-campus recruiting program

- Hired as Assistant Purchasing Manager, served in this capacity from June 2005 to May 2006

- Promoted ahead of schedule to Purchasing Manager; served in this capacity from May 2006 to present

- Promotion to Vice-President (VP) of Operations announced; to be confirmed upon departure of current VP in September 2009

**Professional Accomplishments:**

Assistant Purchasing Manager:

- Managed a $20M widget procurement budget and relationships with 30 suppliers across North America

- Created ABCM's supplier consolidation program, which saved the firm $1.8M in year one

- Initiated ABCM's supplier education program; facilitated three new components, which reduced manual installation and saved 30 man-hours per widget produced

Purchasing Manager:

- Oversaw three Assistant Purchasing Managers and a total budget of $75M; managed relationships with all suppliers (number reduced as a result of consolidation program)

- Applied consolidation program to other two units within firm, generating savings of $5M in other departments

- Mentored three Assistant Purchasing managers; instituted the ABCM Educational Excellence Program (monthly events continue)

- Initiated and facilitated company hedging program, ensuring predictability of inputs (mixed financial results—saved $500K in copper costs; lost $750K in aluminum)

Vice-President of Operations:

- Will join executive team; first nonfamily member to join team

- Will manage the four-member purchasing team and the 40-member manufacturing division

Accomplishments Beyond Professional Responsibilities:

- Started employee recognition program

- Plays on company softball team

# *Sample Recommendation*

1. What is your relationship to, and how long have you known, the applicant? Is this person still employed by your organization (Yes/No)? If "No," when did he/she depart (e.g., August 1999)?[1]

As President of ABC Metals, I represent the second generation of leadership within this family-owned and -managed widget manufacturer. With my son and daughter, who both serve on the executive team, I have been working diligently to cut costs and become more competitive to reinvigorate our firm.[2] It was in this spirit that we decided that we would no longer promote from within, but would institute a college hiring program to ensure that we had "fresh blood."[3] After conducting 20 on-campus interviews[4] for an Assistant Purchasing Manager (APM)[5] at Local State Engineering University, we narrowed our list of candidates to two, and then, after a series of addi-

---

1 You will notice that almost all of the bullet points from the Background section have been incorporated into this letter.
2 Here the recommender introduces himself, his position and the firm.
3 It is worth noting that your recommendations will not be checked for grammar or style. Although it would be more appropriate here to write "to ensure that we brought 'fresh blood' into the company," this wording still gets the central point across, and this is not something the admissions committee will worry about.
4 This reference reveals the depth of the selection process and introduces a comparative element, where the MBA candidate distinguishes himself from others.
5 Ideally, any abbreviations your recommender uses in his/her responses should be written out the first time they appear, to avoid any confusion or missing information for the admissions committee.

tional interviews and even some psychological and aptitude tests, ultimately chose to hire Steve Smith. As you will learn, this was a turning point for our company. Since Steve joined our firm in June 2005, he has helped energize our company and has earned a promotion to Purchasing Manager and is patiently waiting to transition into his VP Operations role[1] this summer. Because our management team is small, I am able to be a "hands-on" leader and thus know Steve's work quite well.[2]

2. Provide a short list of adjectives that describe the applicant's strengths.

Entrepreneurial, innovative, intelligent, thoughtful, driven[3]

3. How does the applicant's performance compare with that of his or her peers?

Steve joined us as an APM and was junior to the other two APM's,[4] who each had seven years of experience with our firm. In fairness, Steve was a college-educated engineer, and our other two APMs did not have similar educational opportunities, but regardless, they were his peers, and he quickly outshone them. In only his third month[5] with the firm, Steve persuaded my son, daughter and me that we needed a revolution in our purchasing program. Rather than spreading our orders to weaken our suppliers' influence over costs, we needed to consolidate and reduce the number of our suppliers to strengthen their dedication to us and eliminate duplication of expenses on our end. Steve's approach saved us $1.8M[6] in our first year, and I quickly promoted him to Purchasing Manager (PM), unfortunately at the cost of ushering out a veteran manager.[7] As PM, Steve again shone, implementing

---

1 Offering such facts proves the candidate's success via promotions.
2 This statement legitimizes the recommender's position to evaluate the candidate.
3 Keeping this kind of list succinct keeps it from becoming overwhelming—and fewer adjectives are more meaningful. The MBA candidate cannot truly be everything, so too many adjectives can undermine the candidate.
4 This is a small issue, but note that this apostrophe is not appropriately placed. This should simply read APMs, because it is plural rather than possessive. However, remember that with regard to recommendations, the admissions committee is worried about content, not grammar.
5 The recommender offers this immediate anecdote to back up the claim that Steve "outshone" his peers.
6 This fact offers clear and tangible results of Steve's efforts.
7 This sobering note shows that the recommender is not offering only "sunshine."

his consolidation program across all three divisions and saving our firm an additional $5M.[8] Steve was the only PM and thus had no peer in this position; when he assumes the title of VP Operations this summer, he will replace an individual who is retiring after a 30-year career and will become the first nonfamily member ever to join the executive team.[9] Clearly, Steve has been promoted well ahead of schedule at our firm and has excelled beyond any reasonable peer group (new college hires or veteran managers) at our firm.

4.  How has the applicant grown during his/her employment with you? Please comment on the applicant's maturity.

In my opinion, it takes a distinctly mature individual to walk into an established family culture and suggest change, all without threatening or alienating others. I have already mentioned Steve's supplier consolidation program, a concept that changed our operations internally as well as our relationship with all of our suppliers. I was profoundly impressed that Steve proactively anticipated the "emotional" effects the consolidation program would have on our remaining suppliers,[10] who might fear being phased out later on, and thus emphasized for them their importance to us by starting the supplier education program. It took tremendous maturity and forward thinking to hold mutual "teach-ins" on a continuous basis at both parties' locations to integrate these suppliers and ensure that we established confidence in them. Since Steve established this program, our relationships have never been stronger—we now truly work *with* our suppliers, and innovations have actually sprung forth from our closer collaboration. Today, Steve represents our firm with our 25 suppliers (down from 70 when he started)—needless to write, a position that requires tremendous maturity and judgment, and one in which he has truly excelled.[11]

---

8  This additional anecdote provides further evidence of candidate's success, and is followed by a comparative element.

9  Again, this recommender can distinguish the candidate as a "first," thereby validating his claim that Steve "outshone" all others.

10 Again, the recommender offers anecdotal evidence to support a claim, in this case maturity. This story demonstrates the individual's level of emotional intelligence.

11 The recommender provides very thorough anecdotal evidence throughout this paragraph, and follows with quantifiable facts (e.g., "Steve represents our firm with our 25 suppliers").

With respect to growth, I have already noted the promotions that Steve has and will receive and the two programs he has initiated at our firm. Beyond these quantifiable indicators, Steve's growth can be observed qualitatively, as he has developed from an individual initiator into an effective manager, who develops others' talents. Steve now manages three APMs and does so with a sense of altruism and magnanimity that we all admire. He is always willing to educate others and started our ABCM Educational Excellence Series, leading sessions personally and bringing in guest speakers on Total Quality Management.[1] Steve has transitioned from an individual bubbling with ideas to a leader who, humbly, facilitates discussions, offers his own ideas to be critiqued by others and encourages others to make distinct contributions.

5. Comment on the applicant's ability to work with others, including superiors, peers and subordinates. If the tables were reversed, would you enjoy working for the applicant?

As I just noted, Steve is excited about developing his team and has been an excellent facilitator for it, so much so that he will soon gain responsibility for the 40-member manufacturing team as well. Steve's humility is his hallmark—he treats everyone with courtesy, respect and inclusion, whether he is establishing educational or employee recognition programs or taking his place as the *worst* player on our company softball team.[2] Steve is constantly thinking of the company and others, recognizing that his growth and the firm's growth depend on a collective. Indeed, he has quite literally broken down the walls in the purchasing department, which has not only saved valuable space, but has also, and more importantly, enhanced communication and promoted a feeling of unity among his team. He no longer has a "privileged" office but is "one of the guys."[3] If the tables were turned, I would enjoy working for such a magnanimous and altruistic leader.

---

1 The recommender legitimizes his claims about the candidate ("developed from an individual initiator into an effective manager") by relaying an anecdote about the candidate educating others.
2 This humorous jab shows that the recommender knows the candidate well and has genuine affection for him, but is not focused on conveying only positives.
3 Again, anecdotal evidence substantiates the claim that Steve is a team player, "constantly thinking of the company and others."

6. In what ways could the applicant improve professionally? How does he/she accept constructive criticism?[4]

I think that we were all impressed with Steve's successes with his consolidation program and educational series and simply expected his success to continue. Frankly speaking, his suggestion that we start a hedging program to gain predictability in our copper and aluminum costs was premature. We were not sophisticated enough for these programs, as we did not have the financial expertise to execute them and lost a few hundred thousand dollars (we were briefly exposed to more than $1 million dollars in potential additional costs). I made the final decision to go ahead; after our first six-month term, I cancelled the program and led a reevaluation with my son, daughter and Steve. During this "postmortem," I was clear with Steve that, as much as it seems nonsensical, it can be naïve to push the firm too far too fast and that his projections were somewhat naïve, as he had not taken into account a true worst case scenario. It was clear to me that Steve was chagrined and indeed, he went back and reran his numbers, increasing the range of potential crises and quickly determined that the program brought far too many risks to our firm in the near term. We have shelved the program for now, and I am eager to see when he proposes it again, as I am sure that he will only present it when we have grown into it. This will indeed be a test of his patience and development. Regardless, I was impressed by his willingness to accept my criticism and to reconsider his own viewpoint. The fact that he went and reran his models and admitted his errors speaks volumes about him.

7. How well has the applicant made use of available opportunities? Consider his or her initiative, curiosity and motivation.

I have offered several examples throughout this letter of initiatives and programs that Steve has undertaken (employee recognition, ABCM Educational

---

4 The recommender's answer here is frank and blunt, but it is not damaging. It reveals the recommender as honest and thoughtful, not just a "cheerleader" who refuses to consider the candidate objectively. While the criticism may "hurt" a little bit, it is not harmful. This is not character assassination, but rather the story of a tough lesson learned.

Excellence, supplier consolidation and supplier education). His spirit of initiative, curiosity and motivation drive him in a way that I have not seen in my 30 years as president, observing both my own firm and many suppliers and customers. These traits, coupled with humility, are Steve's hallmarks, and they are what make him a uniquely capable individual. In hindsight, Steve was not really given any opportunities and yet he seems to have created so many. When we started our college hiring program, we did not expect that we would hire someone who would become the first nonfamily member of our executive team, and admittedly, it was not because we developed Steve but because we got out of the way and let him go, that this was such a success.[1]

8.   Comment on your observations of the applicant's ethical behavior.

When Steve first proposed the supplier consolidation program, it was clear to me that he had considered the effects on all parties. He was not only concerned with dollars and cents, but also clearly understood that we had longstanding relationships with our suppliers, and that these would be affected. Further, he was very cognizant that we would become much bigger customers for several small businesses and was concerned about the risks to them. With Steve, I established protocols for dealing with suppliers, including rules stating that we cannot represent more than 15% of a supplier's sales, for fear that it will be too difficult for us to take away business, as too many lives would be dependent on us.[2] We also agreed that we would give any firm at least six months, and preferably one year, to adjust if we were to remove any business, after implementing our first round of consolidations. I was impressed by the way Steve considered multiple stakeholders and stopped to develop a code of conduct before we implemented—an indication of high ethical values.

---

1   This is a summary statement, as the recommender has already offered specific evidence. The recommender can make strong statements here because he has already backed them up.
2   Again, in this sentence and the next, anecdotal evidence supports the response.

9. What do you think motivates the candidate's application to the MBA program at Columbia Business School? Do you feel the applicant is realistic in his/her professional ambitions?

Because we promoted Steve repeatedly and could see that he was going to be a part of our future, it was imperative that we have open discussions about his potential path.[3] Steve has been determined to pursue an MBA from the start and slowly evolved in his thinking from a part-time MBA to a dedicated two years of study. Even as Steve prepares to join the executive team, we recognize that our firm will have its limitations for him and his growth. In all honesty, the next logical step for him would be to take my position, and I have two family members who are ahead of him in line for the job.[4] Still, we are open to Steve returning and have discussed creating positions for him in the future, maybe even purchasing a smaller manufacturer in a related field for him to manage and integrate.

I recognize that he will go through the recruiting process and that he intends to join a leadership program at a major conglomerate, like General Electric or United Technologies.[5] I think that he is entirely realistic in pursuing these positions, and I would enthusiastically endorse him for them, fully aware of the impact he has had at ABCM.

Steve would benefit immensely from an MBA from Columbia. He has the engineering and operational skills necessary to succeed, but he needs the financial skills and global exposure to excel once again.[6] I have spoken with him about his MBA plans and am certain that this is a well timed decision and that he has very carefully considered his educational options, ultimately choosing Columbia.

---

3 The recommender reveals here how he would have such intimate information about Steve's long-term plans.

4 This fairly blunt statement again reveals the recommender's honesty.

5 This is another very honest statement and shows that there has been open communication throughout and that Steve sets expectations appropriately.

6 It would be unreasonable to expect that this individual possesses intimate knowledge of the CBS MBA program; thus, he does not go into specifics of what the individual will get out of the program beyond the broader recognition of "financial skills and global exposure."

10. Are there any other matters which you feel we should know about the applicant?

I believe I have covered Steve's various merits in the letter above. Should you have any questions, I am certainly available to answer them.[1]

---

1  The recommender is under no obligation to add more information if the important points have been "hit."

# Optional Essays

Chapter 7

# *Optional Essays*

Virtually all top business schools offer applicants the opportunity to address anything unusual or problematic within their profiles. MBA candidates can use either the additional information section of a school's application or the optional essay to *proactively* explain any such irregularities/inconsistencies so that the admissions committee understands the circumstances behind these issues and is not left trying to solve a mystery.

Common reasons to write the optional essay include, but are certainly not limited to, explaining or revealing the following:

- Poor academic performance in a specific class, semester or overall; differences in universities' grading systems

- Low verbal, quantitative or overall GMAT score, or any combination thereof

- Lack of a professional reference due to the candidate's desire not to disclose a potential departure

- Absences from work or college, or gaps in resume

- Academic probation/suspensions, firings or criminal records

By writing an optional essay (remember, the key word here is "optional"; doing so may not be necessary in your case), you will be able to address a problem area in your application and potentially—in the case of poor grades or even a firing—reveal maturity by owning up to mistakes and offering evidence of subsequent growth. We cannot be more deliberate in writing this: *the optional essay is not the place to make excuses or avoid taking responsibility for a mistake.* By attempting to avoid responsibility, you will only compound your problems, revealing that you lack the maturity necessary to contribute to your target MBA program and to be a self-reflective manager capable of continuous professional growth.

If you choose to write an optional essay to address a specific problem, do not take a minimalist approach and present only the problem itself. For example, you should not simply note that you have a low quantitative GMAT score and write that you feel it does not represent your abilities—the admissions committee already knows your results from your score report, and merely expressing your dissatisfaction with the score does not give the school any more information with which to evaluate you. Instead, you will ideally be able to declare that you truly do have the quantitative skills necessary to succeed in business school, show evidence of these skills and then demonstrate that you can indeed contribute via your quantitative abilities (see Sample Essay A in the GMAT Scores section for an example).

> *Tuck Optional Essay: Please provide any additional insight or information that you have not addressed elsewhere that may be helpful in reviewing your application (e.g., unusual choice of evaluators, weaknesses in academic performance, unexplained job gaps or changes, etc.). Complete this question only if you feel your candidacy is not fully represented by this application.*

> *Chicago Optional Essay: If there is any important information that is relevant for your candidacy that you were unable to address elsewhere in the application, please share that information here.*

> *Yale School of Management Optional Essay: If any aspect of your candidacy needs further explanation, please provide any additional information that you would like the admissions committee to consider. (250 words maximum)*

By the time the admissions officer who reads your application gets to your optional essay, he/she will have already gone through much, if not all, of the rest of your application. Also, keep in mind that he/she will likely have read dozens, if not hundreds, of other applications and essays as well. So, try to put yourself in the admissions officer's position—applications are piling up and you are doing your best to ensure that each applicant gets your full attention, but you have a lot of work ahead of you and somewhat repetitious work at that. Our point is that by submitting an optional essay, you are essentially asking the admissions officer to read another essay—basically, to do even more work. So, the key to writing an effective optional essay is to respect this individual's time and be *as brief as possible, while still conveying all the necessary information.*

In a personal essay, it is generally unwise to write less than the word limit—you want to be as thorough as possible in answering the school's question. In an optional essay, however, you may not have a word limit, but it is crucial to be concise. We recommend limiting yourself to four to eight sentences per topic that you feel needs to be addressed. Writing just 150 words is perfectly acceptable, and in fact is preferred, even if your target MBA program gives you a 250- or 500-word limit.

In light of our earlier statement about staying on point and respecting admissions officers' time, the optional essay is absolutely *not* the place to include an essay that you think really portrays you positively, but that you were not otherwise able to use for this particular school. By pasting in an essay you originally wrote for another school, you will reveal only that you have followed instructions. You will not gain any additional "points" for telling one more story than anyone else, and an overworked admissions officer will only be frustrated by having to read and evaluate another essay that is not relevant to his/her decision. The officer will either ignore the essay altogether or read it in its entirety, waiting for some bit of crucial information that never actually comes. Neither scenario is positive.

Also, it is important to repeat that you *do not need* to write an optional essay; you are certainly not disadvantaged if you have no information to share via this space. If your grades are solid and your GPA is based on a typical scale and your GMAT scores are balanced and you have naturally progressed in your career and you have… (you get the point), then writing an optional essay is not essential for you. If you have had no such "blips" in your academic and professional history and no mysteries are lurking in your file, you should consider yourself fortunate, leave the optional essay space blank and move on.

# Academic Issues

For an MBA candidate to have a spotless academic transcript is surprisingly rare. In this section we offer instances in which you might consider writing an optional essay, though this list is not meant to be comprehensive or cover all academic scenarios. There is always room for judgment, of course, and candidates are urged to use discretion when writing optional statements.

- If your undergraduate GPA is weak (generally understood to be anything less than a 3.0 [or converted equivalent]), you should submit an optional essay that explains your performance and, more importantly, offers evidence that you are now prepared to excel academically.

- If you had a particularly poor semester or year(s) but still earned a GPA of 3.0 or higher, you should consider writing an optional essay to explain the temporary downshift in your academic performance. However, do not confuse one or two low grades with a poor semester or term. If you had one C in your second semester one year but otherwise earned a 3.75 GPA, you probably should not write the optional essay.

- If you had any failing grades at all (i.e., you earned an F [or equivalent] as your final grade in a class), you will need to use the optional essay to explain why and how this happened. We have seen candidates recover from an F or two—doing so is not unheard of.

- If you performed poorly in quantitative classes (statistics, calculus) or management classes (finance, accounting), you should explain your current aptitude in these areas. Ideally, you will have since bolstered your qualifications in these areas via additional classes or professional experiences that prove your competencies, and these should be clearly presented in the optional essay.

- If you were put on academic probation or suspended at any time, you should explain the circumstances surrounding the situation in your optional essay and, more importantly, present what you learned from the experience.

- If you repeatedly switched majors throughout college and, as a result, your transcript tells a muddled story, you should consider using the optional essay to explain your path.

- If your GPA in absolute terms is relatively low but in relative terms puts you in the top of your class, the optional essay is a great way to clarify this and help the Admissions Committee view your academic record in a more positive light. For example, the chemical engineer from India who has a 68% overall yet finished at the top of his/her class would want to explain that his/her GPA should be considered in context. Similarly, if your GPA conversion requires explanation because it is based on a different scale, you can use the optional essay to convey the differences.

Optional Essays

## Sample Essays

A) *When I arrived at ABC University, I made a significant error in judgment by committing myself to my fraternity rather than to my academics. At the end of my first year, I was shocked by my 1.9 GPA and was fortunately "scared straight." During my sophomore year, I carefully selected my major, economics, and was conscientious in choosing my courses, identifying those that were interesting and challenging to me. Simply put, I then spent my weeknights in the library, ensuring that my abysmal first year would not have an encore. At the end of my second year, even though I had started volunteering as a Big Brother in addition to fulfilling my fraternity responsibilities, I earned a 3.6 GPA. Thereafter, my GPA continued to improve as I earned a 3.7 in my junior year and a 3.9 in my senior year, while also serving as president of my fraternity, maintaining my volunteer commitments and serving as student representative on the hiring panel for the economics department. In the end, my overall GPA was a 3.3, but I feel that my final three years are a true indication of my abilities and of the individual I am today—one who thrives with multiple responsibilities and performs when challenged.* (See Sample Essay A in the What Not to Write section at the end of this chapter for an example of how *not* to address the identical circumstances.)

Why is this essay effective? The writer is honest and direct, quickly taking responsibility for his actions by stating that he made a "significant error in judgment." The individual then tells the story of his improvement and also shows that he was capable of maintaining his external interests at the same time—proving that he did not need to forsake his commitments to achieve balance in his life. Further, the individual convincingly states that he should be judged on his final years by revealing the obvious disparity between his first year at college and his final three years.

You may have read this and said to yourself, "Ok, but what if there was no recovery? What if my improvement was minimal at best?" Well, many of the same principles—being contrite and offering evidence of subsequent maturity—still apply.

B) *It has been four years since I graduated with a 2.7 GPA and a degree in biology. In hindsight, it is clear even to me that I lacked the maturity at the time to grasp the opportunities before me. Two years ago, I enrolled in ABC University's extension program, where I have taken "Accounting I" and "Corporate Finance I," earning As in both classes. More recently, I have spread my wings and taken "French Film and Literature" and "The Novels of Dickens," earning an A in the first and a B+ in the second. I realize now that during my undergraduate days, I squandered an intellectual opportunity; now I am focused and am pursuing education for its own sake—making up for lost time. Today, as a twice-promoted brand manager at ABC Corp., I know that I have grown and identified professional and intellectual passions. I am looking forward to two years at XYZ Business School, where I intend not only to perform, but also to seize every opportunity to expand my intellectual horizons.*

Why is this essay effective? Again, the writer takes responsibility and then reveals evidence of change. Further, he offers proof of maturity via professional advancement, reinforcing the claim of having changed, and states that he looks forward to attending business school because of the both academic and intellectual opportunity it offers—adding a dose of balance and sincerity. He is studying not just for the sake of his GPA but for himself.

In some cases, an individual will actually have a legitimate rationale for poor academic performance, such as a serious illness or significant work demands. In such cases, the candidate should simply tell the story of how his/her studies were disrupted by the issue, as in the example that follows.

Optional Essays

C) *My parents, neither of whom graduated from high school, never encouraged me to go to college and saved nothing for my education. I attended ABC University because it offered me a partial scholarship, but I still needed to work 40 hours per week to cover my remaining tuition and living expenses. I take great pride in the fact that I worked two ten-hour shifts at Gimli Furniture on the weekends as an hourly salesperson and then worked four hours each weekday as well. During my summers, I worked overtime, often 60 hours per week, so that I could take some of the pressure off during my academic year. I am certain that my 2.9 GPA would have been higher had I worked less and studied more, but that was not an option for me, and ultimately, I became the first in my family to earn a college degree. I graduated debt free and still keep my Gimli name tag on my desk as a humble reminder of how far I have come.*

Why is this essay effective? The writer offers a powerful personal story that clearly explains why his performance should be viewed through a different lens than most candidates' records. He does not ask for sympathy or tell a drawn-out sob story but instead presents his academic performance with dignity and pride. The admissions committee is not asked to pity this individual but is implicitly told that this person is driven and can be expected to succeed going forward.

Sometimes, when a candidate is dealing with technical issues, he/she can take a straightforward approach to an optional essay, as in the following example.

D) *I have converted my GPA using XYZ Business School's suggested scale. Thus, my 80% overall translates to a B average. Given that the records office's Web site states that grades of 80% are given to the top 10% of the class and 90% to the top 1%, I feel that my 80% (or B average) may understate my performance. I cannot provide guidance for what an appropriate conversion of my percentage might be, but I do ask that the admissions committee consider my academic performance with this context in mind.*

Why is this essay effective? This is a very technical issue, and the writer quickly breaks down the components and explains why his grades need special interpretation. He does not belabor the point; nor does he express anxiety or concern for what the alternative conversion might bring. He simply presents the issue for the admissions committee's consideration and moves on.

# GMAT Scores

Generally, the benchmark for a worry-free GMAT score is a balanced 80th percentile on both the quantitative and verbal sections of the test and a 700 overall. If you have a 79th percentile on one section or a 690 overall, however, you should not panic, especially if you have evidence in your transcript and/or work experience that shows that you can handle the rigors of a heavily analytical and quantitative curriculum. When deciding whether writing an optional essay would be worthwhile with regard to your GMAT score, consider your GPA and work experiences as well. That written, we generally advise candidates to address their GMAT results if they have scored below the 75th percentile or less than 660 overall, though there are always exceptions.

## Sample Essays

A) *After accepting my score on my first GMAT, I was pleased by my 700 overall but surprised to see a low quantitative score of 66th percentile. (My verbal score was 95th percentile.) I have long considered my quantitative and analytical abilities strengths, evidenced by my having completed all three levels of the Chartered Financial Analyst exam on the first try, my As in statistics and calculus as an undergrad and my two years as an investment banker, where I am immersed in analysis each day. I hope that, for now, the admissions committee will recognize that my low quantitative score is an anomaly. I will be retaking the test on December 9th and will apprise you of my progress. Regardless of the outcome of this future test, I am confident that given my educational and professional experiences, I will be able to effectively manage ABC*

*University's challenging MBA curriculum and contribute to my learning team and to classroom conversations.*

B) *I have taken the GMAT four times, and to my dismay, and clearly not because of a lack of determination, I seem unable to score higher than a 630 overall. Unfortunately, my best scores on each section of the test—a 77% on the quantitative section and a 71% on the verbal section— did not occur on the same day, and my scores have fluctuated with each try. I am disappointed to be applying with an overall score that is well under ABC University's average. I earned As in accounting, economics and finance as an undergraduate and know that I have the aptitude and intellectual abilities to perform in your MBA program.*

Why are these essays effective? Unlike discussing problems with your GPA, you really cannot offer a lengthy backstory with regard to a low GMAT score. Your GMAT score is reflective of a moment in time, not a process that began when you were 18 or 19 and lasted several years. So, you can show effort in taking the GMAT and in trying to improve your score, and then do your best to show other, related areas where you have shined at other times.

You will notice that in Example A here in particular, the writer is able to show a prolonged track record of academic and professional success in quantitative areas, enabling him to potentially mitigate the effects of the low quantitative score. In the second example, the evidence is not as profound, but the attempt is still equally important. The second individual's target school will need to know that he can succeed in the program and then will have to consider the quality of his experiences as it makes its decision. Remember, an optional essay is not a cure-all, but rather an opportunity to proactively address certain problems or weaknesses so that the admissions committee has complete information as it makes its decision.

# Lack of Professional Reference

It is not uncommon for candidates to lack a recommendation from a direct supervisor. As Harvard Business School (HBS) Admissions Director Dee Leopold explains, you should not worry that you are disadvantaged if you don't have a current supervisor writing one of your recommendations:

> *"Please don't jeopardize your employment in order to secure a recommendation from a current employer. While we might wish that all bosses were enthusiastic and encouraging about business school for their emerging leaders, this is not a universal sentiment. Make your best judgment call about whom to ask, make sure they understand what we're asking, explain your choices to us if you think you should… and that's it!"*

*—July 20, 2009, HBS Admissions Blog*

As Ms. Leopold notes, you should explain why you do not have a recommendation from your direct supervisor and make sure the admissions committee knows the reasons behind your alternative selections.

## Sample Essay

A) *I have elected not to inform my firm of my desire to pursue my MBA, because I believe doing so may adversely affect my year-end bonus and possibly even my employment with the company.*

*Rather than asking my current manager to write on my behalf, I have asked my former manager, David Stephenson, with whom I worked closely for two years as Assistant Brand Manager (ABM) to his Brand Manager at ABC Corp., to write a recommendation for me. During my time at ABC, I progressed from intern to ABM and thus developed from a researcher to a decision maker, all on Mr. Stephenson's watch. Mr. Stephenson supervised me during a very formative part of my career and*

197

*ceased to be my manager eight months ago, when I transitioned to my current firm. I am confident that his opinion is still quite relevant and indeed profound.*

*I have also asked Steve Jones, my relationship manager at QRS Ltd.—my firm's most significant client—to share his insights on my performance as well. I have worked with Mr. Jones on an almost daily basis for eight months, speaking with him about purchasing decisions, and I am the only person from outside his company who attends his monthly planning meetings, where I help manage his purchases. I feel that Mr. Jones knows my professional abilities well and will offer a sincere appraisal of my skills.*

Why is this essay effective? In short, it is a very straightforward essay wherein the writer clearly conveys all the necessary information. The essay is simple in that it explains first why a letter is not being sought from the writer's current supervisor and then addresses his alternative choices, offering clear reasons as to why these individuals are qualified to provide a recommendation.

# Absences from Work or College, or Gaps in Resume

The admissions committee does not expect each and every applicant to have progressed along a clear track to business school from day one of their professional careers to today. If you have taken time off from work or have a gap in your resume due to personal reasons, use the optional essay as an opportunity to simply address this absence head on. Again, make no excuses and leave no mysteries!

## Sample Essays

A) *As a 22-year-old college graduate, I took a chance and declined a job offer from a consulting firm, choosing instead to travel the world. For the next 14 months—essentially until I exhausted myself—I ran a hostel in Peru to finance my travels in South America, served as an English-speaking tour guide in Prague to extend my travels into Eastern Europe and performed manual labor on a farm in New Zealand to be able to explore the Asia-Pacific region. During this time, I learned enough Spanish to hike four days to Machu Picchu and spend eight days sailing through the Galapagos, all with Spanish tour guides; I milked cows and goats two hours north of Auckland and learned to surf on Australia's Bell's Beach. I also met people from practically every country in the world while I led tours of "Baroque Prague" and later travelled with four of my tour attendees to Red Square and the Hermitage. Needless to write, perhaps, taking those 14 months to see the world was one of the best decisions of my life. I returned home with remarkable memories, experiences and friends around the world, but also with a resolve. I was fortunate to return during a boom time, and my firm unexpectedly extended me a job offer, which I accepted. I appreciated the firm's loyalty and have attempted to pay it back through hard work. Since joining ABC Consulting in the fall of 2006, I have been promoted ahead of schedule and continue to take on more responsibilities. I have satiated my wanderlust for now—though I know travel will always be a part of my life—and am a better employee, co-worker and person for having pursued these adventures.*

B) *Much to my surprise, during a routine checkup halfway through my first year as an analyst at XYZ Firm, I was diagnosed with cancer. My company quickly granted me an extended leave of absence, and I returned home to start chemotherapy and radiation treatments. Although the treatments were grueling, I responded quite well to them and was able to return to the firm after seven months away. Today, as I work 16-hour days, like others at the company, I frequently remind myself how lucky I am that there is no longer any sign of cancer in my body. Despite the rigors of my schedule—no matter what—I volunteer my time at the local hospital, reading to children in the cancer ward, and I fundraise for the hospital's yearly Walk for the Cure. January 13, 2011, is already circled on my calendar. That is the day I will officially be declared cancer free, but I intend to maintain my charitable commitments until we see a medical breakthrough.*

C) *Like many in the financial community, I never imagined a day when Bear Stearns would cease to exist. What seemed to be the safest position in the world to me clearly was not, and I was laid off from my position as Analyst with Bear Stearns in the spring of 2008. Of course, finding a new position in the financial field was very difficult at that time, because there was a glut of highly skilled investment banking analysts looking for employment, and firms were not hiring. I took a disciplined approach and sent my resume to three firms in the financial field each day, but as the crisis intensified, I knew that I was facing longer and longer odds of reestablishing myself in New York on Wall Street. In the meantime, I started to volunteer at a local elementary school, teaching math in an after-school program and mentoring budding entrepreneurs through Junior Achievement. I also started to look for small firms outside New York and again, sending out no less than three resumes a day, I remained optimistic. I eventually took a position with Smith Bros., a small asset management firm in Minneapolis, in the spring of 2009. I have truly enjoyed the opportunity to transition to the buy side of finance, and even though it took 11 months, I feel fortunate to have landed on my feet as the market remains challenging.*

Why are these essays effective? Each statement is different, yet each one very clearly and deliberately explains the writer's unique circumstances and how the individual dealt with opportunity/adversity. Further, each essay reveals that the writer learned a great deal from the situation and grew significantly during the time away from the professional world.

# Academic Probation/Suspensions, Firings or Criminal Records

There is probably no instance in which our "make no excuses and leave no mysteries" mantra is more applicable than those in which candidates are dealing with academic probation, suspensions, firings or criminal records. Here, more than anywhere else, you must take complete responsibility for your past actions and show subsequent growth.

## Sample Essays

A) *I will never forget December 12, 2004—the day I pleaded no contest to driving under the influence of alcohol.*

*Six months prior, I made a choice that I will always regret, driving home after watching football at a friend's on a Sunday afternoon. When I saw the officer's flashing lights in the rearview mirror, I pulled over and was completely shaken as he explained that I was fortunate to have not hurt anyone and that he was worried not about me but others. It was when he pointed out how I had put other people in danger with my choices that the stupidity of my actions truly hit home.*

*I lost my driver's license for six months. Each time I took the bus—four times a day—during those six months, I was reminded of my error. I was sentenced to 100 hours of community service and completed those hours in three months, even though the judge had mandated a six-month time frame, volunteering with Mothers Against Drunk Driving (MADD). I continue to work with MADD to this day, speaking to school groups about my experience and helping in the local chapter's office, stuffing envelopes or completing data entry.*

*I have not had a drink since the day I was pulled over. It seems like a lifetime ago, because I was very much a different person then. I made an awful mistake, but I have definitely changed.*

Why is this essay effective? The writer is clearly contrite, offering sincere regret and showing considerable change, with evidence (volunteer work) to support and illustrate this claim. Any balanced reader should accept this statement and recognize that this individual has grown as a result of the experience and is indeed quite different today.

B) *I was unsure what I wanted to do upon graduation from ABC University and took a sales position with a software reselling firm simply because, quite frankly, it was offered to me in an on-campus interview. At the time, I had no other plans, and repayment of my student loans was looming on the horizon. I was unsure whether joining MicroChoices was the right move, and within a few weeks of my start date, it had become clear to me that I was a poor fit with the company. Although I enjoyed the human interaction that comes with sales and felt that MicroChoices had integrity, I just did not feel passionately about the firm's products and services. After six months, I was in the lowest quartile in terms of my sales performance, and I was let go.*

*I know that my dismissal was not personal—it was part of a numbers game, and my numbers clearly did not measure up. I also know that as someone who has never quit anything, I likely would have stayed in the position indefinitely and tried to make it work, even though it ultimately did not. I don't write this whimsically, but being fired was a blessing, because it was key to getting me on the right professional path.*

*For the next six months, I lived with my parents so I could lower my overhead and remove any pressure to take the wrong job just to have a paycheck. I completed more than 20 informational interviews in ten different industries and subsequently started sending out resumes in the digital media sales space. I joined MacroChoice Media after five interviews and three lunches with potential team members and have felt comfortable in my role with the company from day one. I am confident that my job performance—as evidenced by my promotion and reflected in my recommendations—demonstrates that this time I have made a mature choice and learned significantly from my original post-graduate work experience.*

Why is this essay effective? The writer focuses on explaining why he and the first company were a poor fit and does not cast stones about a lack of support or a tumultuous relationship with his boss. He tells the story of what he liked and did not like about the original job and how he has since converted this negative situation into a true learning experience. This sample essay is somewhat longer than our other examples, but the writer's story required additional explanation (remember, there is always room for judgment). If you cannot reflect sincerely after being fired—if you can find no profound rationale for why your termination was a learning experience—then your essay will not be effective, and admissions committees will have difficulty finding you very appealing as a potential student. This essay writer is contrite but thoughtful, and the individual's learning and growth are evident throughout.

# What Not to Write

We have elected to offer here a few examples of what you should **not** write in an optional essay. You may be tempted to laugh at these examples, but these are loosely based on actual essays that we have received over the years.

## Sample Essays

A) *When I was in college, I was very devoted to extracurricular activities. I was the president of my fraternity and volunteered as a Big Brother, activities that took 20 hours per week. During my freshman year, I was so busy with my fraternity that I had trouble balancing my studies, and*

*I finished the year with a 1.9 GPA. Thereafter, I improved dramatically, and I finished my college career with a 3.3 overall.*

What is wrong with this essay? Extracurricular involvements are used an excuse for the writer's poor academic performance—absolutely no soul-searching or maturity is displayed here. Clearly, many individuals work to put themselves through school or volunteer actively and are still able to perform at a high level academically. This writer's social schedule did not prevent him from achieving academically. He prevented himself from doing so by choosing instead to spend his time away from his studies. (See a counterexample in Sample Essay A in the Academic Issues section.)

B) *I scored a 710 on my GMAT and feel that this is not indicative of my potential…*

What is wrong with this essay statement? The optional essay is not the place to explain that a strong performance could have been even stronger. The individual who writes such an essay reveals that he/she lacks humility and self-awareness, which will certainly not ingratiate the writer to the admissions committee.

C) *My 2.9 GPA is not indicative of my academic abilities. As an undergrad, I was not focused on my studies. Going forward, I will take advantage of all academic opportunities before me. I know that I have the intellectual abilities to succeed and will do so while studying at XYZ University's MBA program. I anticipate that I will be an XYZ Scholar and will do my utmost to achieve this distinction.*

What is wrong with this essay? Although the writer reveals good intentions going forward, the essay lacks any clear evidence that the individual has changed in any way and does nothing to prove that the writer truly has the "intellectual abilities to succeed." As in any compelling essay, the writer's claims need to be proven anecdotally. Has this individual taken additional classes to bolster his/her capabilities and get back into the routine of course work, for example? Or, has this person excelled professionally in a pure management position? No such information has been offered to the reader. Further, the individual's boast that he/she anticipates becoming an XYZ Scholar seems not only unfounded, of course, but also a bit silly at this stage and completely unnecessary.

Optional Essays

# Interviews

Chapter 8

# *Interviews*

## Types of Interviews

The MBA interview can take on a variety of forms. Some business schools allow for applicant-initiated interviews and offer candidates the opportunity to schedule an interview at their leisure, while other interviews are school initiated, meaning the admissions office will extend an interview invitation (or not extend one) to selected applicants after reading their applications. Some schools even employ a hybrid model, wherein before the application deadline for a round, candidates can request and complete an interview. After the deadline, however, interviews are by invitation only.

Once your interview has been scheduled with your target school, the person who will conduct your interview can vary from program to program. Some admissions offices conduct all candidate interviews themselves either on campus or in hub cities across the United States and foreign countries, while others will ask students or alumni to conduct interviews in person or even over the phone. (Recently, some schools have even experimented with Skype.) Another differentiator is that at some schools, the interview will be "comprehensive," meaning that your interviewer will have read your entire application cover to cover (usually more than once!) before your meeting, whereas at others, your interview will be "blind," meaning that the interviewer will have seen only your resume and thus will not know your GMAT score or GPA (unless, of course, this information is on your resume) or the content of your essays. Regardless of the venue or the person interviewing you, your goal remains the same; to communicate your distinct attributes and prove that you have the personality to support the standout application you have already submitted. In the following tables, we present information on the types of admissions interviews conducted by top U.S. business schools. (Note: Data in these tables are based on information available on each school's Web site at the time of publication.)

Interview

### Table A

| School | Interview Process | | Interview Type | |
|---|---|---|---|---|
| | Invitation | Applicant Initiated | Blind | Comprehensive |
| Chicago Booth | • | | • | |
| Columbia Business School | • | | • | |
| Cornell Johnson | • | | • | |
| Dartmouth Tuck | • | • | • | |
| Duke Fuqua | • | • | • | |
| Harvard Business School | • | | | • |
| Michigan Ross | • | | • | |
| MIT Sloan | • | | | • |
| Northwestern Kellogg | • | • | • | |
| NYU Stern | • | | | • |
| Stanford GSB | • | | • | |
| UCLA Anderson | • | | • | |
| UC-Berkeley Haas | • | | • | |
| UPenn Wharton | • | | • | |
| UVA Darden | • | | • | |
| Yale | • | | • | |

*Table B*

| School | Interviewer | | | Location | |
|---|---|---|---|---|---|
| | Admissions | Alumni | Student | On Campus | Off Campus |
| Chicago Booth | • | • | • | • | • |
| Columbia Business School | | • | | | • |
| Cornell Johnson | • | • | • | • | • |
| Dartmouth Tuck | • | • | • | • | • |
| Duke Fuqua | • | • | • | • | • |
| Harvard Business School | • | • | | • | • |
| Michigan Ross | • | • | • | • | • |
| MIT Sloan | • | | | • | • |
| Northwestern Kellogg | • | • | • | • | • |
| NYU Stern | • | | | • | • |
| Stanford GSB | | • | | | • |
| UCLA Anderson | • | • | • | • | • |
| UC-Berkeley Haas | | • | • | • | • |
| UPenn Wharton | | • | • | • | • |
| UVA Darden | • | | • | • | |
| Yale | • | • | • | • | • |

Interview

# What Will They Ask Me?

The vast majority of MBA interviews are simple and straightforward. Candidates often fear that interviews will be aggressive, but most are relatively friendly "get to know you" sessions, wherein you can expect to be asked questions about your personal and professional history, career goals and reasons for applying to the particular school that is interviewing you. Therefore, try your best to relax. By relaxing, you will enjoy the process more, and you will likely show your best side to your interviewers.

You will almost certainly know the answers to the questions you are asked during the interview, because they will virtually always be about you and your experiences. You will never be asked to explain the theory of relativity or to discuss economic policy in Namibia (unless, perhaps, you happen to be a physicist or a specialist in Namibian economic policy!). Remember, interviews are not tests of your general knowledge or familiarity with a certain subject, but explorations of who you are as an individual and a professional. The best strategy during an interview is to respond in a relaxed manner with the most natural, truthful and direct answer possible to the question asked.

## Types of Questions

### Open-Ended Questions:

Many interviews begin with an open-ended request like "Tell me about yourself," "Walk me through your resume" or "Discuss your career progress since graduating from college." You should answer such open-ended "questions" in three to four minutes at the most. The interviewer only wants the highlights of your life/career, with an emphasis on how you have made decisions, and does not need to hear about each project undertaken in every position you have ever held. If an interviewer is particularly interested in something you mention, he/she will ask follow-up questions and probe deeper.

### Follow-Up Questions:

After the open-ended first question, many interviews proceed with follow-up questions like "What are your short- and long-term goals after graduating with your MBA?" "Why do you need an MBA?" and "Why do you need an MBA from our school?" Generally, you should answer such questions in two to three minutes each. Your responses should be detailed but concise—

though not too concise! Responding to a career question with *"I intend to go into consulting and then pursue an entrepreneurial venture"* is not enough. You should elaborate and offer details, as well as a rationale for why this career suits you and why pursuing these career goals upon graduating with your MBA makes perfect sense, but do so within the recommended two to three minutes. Similarly, when you are asked why you have applied to a particular school, an answer such as *"XYZ School has a great entrepreneurship program and a very small student body,"* for example, would not be sufficient. A persuasive response would cite specific features of the school and display your intimate knowledge of the program's particular benefits and culture: *"When I visited XYZ, I was impressed by the school's commitment to entrepreneurship. The programs offered through the Thompson Center, the Venture Formation Program and the Managers Round Table will offer me precisely the sort of academic experience I am seeking in an MBA program. What's more, I love that the student body is small and intimate."*

Offering a detailed response in two minutes is entirely possible, and the best way to prepare yourself to provide such a response is to refresh yourself on the school's strengths in your area of academic interest and need (in this example, the Thompson Center and its benefits for entrepreneurship) and on the school's culture and reputation (in this example, the small, tightly knit student body) before your interview.

## Targeted Questions:

After about the first four questions, the interviewer will likely ask about your career or extracurricular activities, posing questions like "What are your strengths and weaknesses as a leader?" "Of what accomplishment are you most proud?" and "Discuss a time when you led a team. How were you effective as a leader? What could you have done better?" Again, you should answer such questions in detail but also concisely. You should also always offer real-life examples of your experiences to support any claims you make. Saying *"As a leader I am a strong motivator, a clear communicator and a goal-*

*oriented implementer*" is simply not enough. By providing examples of instances in which you demonstrated such characteristics and skills, you will establish legitimacy for your claims: "*As a leader, I am a strong motivator. I remember that on the XYZ project, morale was quite low because we were dealing with a difficult client. Recognizing the problem, I took the following three steps … . In addition, I am a straightforward communicator. I find that by establishing very clear expectations with my coworkers, I am able to set the agenda in an effective but respectful manner. On one case in particular, our team was … .*" Again, "fleshing out" your claims with real examples drawn from your life makes your answers much more effective and persuasive—not to mention much more interesting.

This second phase of questions will generally be very open and malleable. Candidates may sometimes get flustered because they cannot, for example, come up with their "greatest accomplishment" on the spot. Whether your greatest accomplishment is when you took an entrepreneurial risk or when you raised $10K for charity does not matter—there is no "right" answer. Rather, the key is to respond intelligently, thoughtfully and thoroughly to the question asked.

## Final Questions:

The final phase of the interview often consists of a personal question or two, such as "What do you do for fun?" or "What are your favorite hobbies and activities?" Again, these questions have no wrong answers. Think to yourself how you would answer these questions if one of your friends had asked them. Although these kinds of questions may seem unusual, given that you are focused on your career goals and on getting into a particular MBA program, the answers are still within you and are not difficult to find. Relax, think and answer—and, where appropriate, tie your answer to certain extracurricular activities you could pursue at the school. For instance, if you are asked "How do you most enjoy spending your free time?" a strong answer could be "*I love playing ice hockey—my earliest memories are of skating on the frozen pond at my grandparents' Minnesota farm. I still play twice a week with a group of friends, both because I love the sport and because it is great exercise. In fact, yet another reason I am so excited about attending XYZ School is because of the student hockey team.*" You will notice how this answer is concise yet detailed, how it includes real-life examples and links directly with the school's extracurricular offerings. Constantly relating your experiences to your target school's offerings can become tiresome, however, so be careful not to overdo it and to keep such references relevant and believable.

## Your Questions:

Most interviewers will leave time for you to ask a few questions of them in return. The interview is not the time to learn about the school (you should know the school "inside and out" before you arrive), but rather an opportunity to ask insightful questions that inferentially showcase your knowledge of the school or that show you are critically evaluating your options. For example, this is not the time to ask, "What entrepreneurial programs do you have?" If you are interested in entrepreneurship, you should already know the answer to this question. However, you could ask, for example, "The new dean has been in place for six months now. Would you say that the school has changed in any significant way during this time?" Such a question shows that you are aware of what is taking place on campus and are evaluating the school in part based on this major change—you have not just looked at the school's ranking and made the decision to apply, but have really done your research and considered your options. Avoid overarching exploratory questions ("What should I know about your finance program?") and vague questions with no direct connection to your goals ("What do *you* like about the business school?"), while also keeping in mind who your interviewer is—alumni may not know specifics about recent changes to curriculum or budgets on campus, for example, whereas admissions personnel may not have as much insight into how the MBA comes into play in the workplace (as an alumnus/alumna would).

Interview

Also, be sure to have multiple questions ready for the interviewer to show that you have done more than just the minimum to get by and also so you have backup queries, in case the question you had originally planned to ask is naturally answered during the course of your interview. Take the time and do the homework necessary to ensure that your questions show you are truly knowledgeable about and interested in the school and that they pertain to information you need and genuinely want to know. If you are searching for questions to ask an interviewer, read the school's latest press releases or look for recent news on the school's Web site. Press releases and Web site postings offer a great opportunity for you to learn about important announcements and initiatives. You can also ask the interviewer a relevant question about his or her experience if it relates to your goals. Remember, though, that the questions you formulate using information from these sources should directly relate to you and your candidacy and should not be generic.

## What If I Am Stumped?

Many business school applicants worry that in their interview, they may be asked a single challenging question that leaves them awkwardly silent and that such a moment will be the symbolic end to their candidacy at the school. While such an experience would certainly be uncomfortable—and we suggest, of course, that you definitely do your best to prepare for your interview so as to avoid this kind of predicament—sometimes even well-prepared candidates can be "stumped," and we can assure you that an awkward pause in an interview will not cancel out all the positive elements of your application. Still, being ready for such a situation, should one occur, is key, so we offer the following tips on how to mitigate an awkward moment:

- *Resist the urge to launch into a story:* Your instinct may be to just start speaking, hoping that you will find the right story as you progress. This is a high-risk strategy because, if it goes wrong, it can compound the problem. Instead, you might consider a pensive pause and take a moment to search for the story internally. You might even say,

"That is a good question. I am going to have to think about it for a moment," before answering.

- *Take a sip of water*: Many interviewers will offer you a glass of water at the beginning. Take the water and use it throughout the interview as a buffer to buy time or allow yourself to slow down. If you get stumped, the water can offer a brief opportunity to pause naturally, alleviating any awkwardness before you begin.

- *Maintain your poise*: If you absolutely cannot answer a question, you should not get overly apologetic or grovel. Simply acknowledge the fact that you are having trouble with the question and politely ask if you might come back to it at the end. This is not a best-case scenario, but it is certainly far better than rambling and apologizing.

- *Forget about it*: If you cannot answer a question, accept it and move on. If you spend the rest of the interview thinking about that moment, you will be distracted and struggle with any subsequent questions. If you confidently move on and make the best of the rest of the interview, you should be able to overcome a single awkward moment.

All of that said, you can rest assured that your interviewer is not out to fool you or trick you. As we have noted, most of the questions you will receive should probe your experiences, and getting a question that is designed to trip you up is exceedingly rare.

Consider the following excerpts about the interview process taken from our interviews with the admissions directors of several top U.S. MBA schools:

> *"And it's [our interview] really, I would say, a fairly standard behavioral interview. The purpose is not to trick you or throw curveballs, but really get a sense of the applicant, get a sense of their background, their interests, why they want to get an MBA, what they want to do with their degree."*

*—Bruce DelMonico, Admissions Director, Yale School of Management*

*"Ours [our interviews] are, intentionally, fairly informal. We have interviews that are conducted by our staff as well as alumni and current students, and typically, when someone comes in for an interview, a few minutes are spent just making the person feel at ease. We try to ease people into it. They're definitely not intended to put someone on a hot seat."*

*—Dawna Clarke, Director of MBA Admissions, Dartmouth-Tuck*

*"I advise people to put together the absolute best application you can, and I think a big part of that, as clichéd as this is going to sound, is really just being who you are. Not trying to be who you think we want to read about or who we want to hear in an interview. Just be you."*

*—Beth Flye, Assistant Dean and Director of Admissions and Financial Aid, Northwestern-Kellogg*

*"I would say the overall perspective, and this is true for the interview, but it's true, I think, for the whole process, is a positive perspective. So, we're not looking for reasons to deny someone, we're looking for reasons to admit someone."*

*—J.J. Cutler, Director of MBA Admissions and Financial Aid, University of Pennsylvania-Wharton*

In addition, Chicago Booth's Associate Dean for Student Recruitment and Admissions Rose Martinelli states the following on her blog:

*"Here's the hard part—once you've practiced and prepared, you need to set aside all that preparation so that you can focus on having a conversation with your interviewer. Remember, the interviewer knows Booth well, but not you. So feel free to allow the conversation to be two way.*

*Getting to know the person sitting across the table will help you to relax and relate your stories more effectively."*

# How Do I Prepare?

## Know Your Story

The first rule of any MBA interview is *Know your story*. Most interviews take place several months after you have submitted your application. We strongly recommend that before your interview, you reacquaint yourself with your story as you submitted it to the school: review your resume, essays and application form so that you are prepared to discuss your ambitions, experiences and all the other details and themes you presented in your application documents. You should be able to discuss with ease the three or four top reasons for which (1) you want/need an MBA at this point of your life and (2) you want to go to the school for which you are interviewing.

## Time Management

During your interview, time management is critical. Interviews are typically 30 minutes long, and most interviewers will have a list of questions prepared (maybe not a physical list before them, but at least a mental agenda), and they want to get through their entire list in the time allotted. If you ramble on and take eight minutes to answer a single question, for example, you could give the interviewer the impression that you lack self-awareness and may talk too much in class. Using up time in this way also limits the interviewer's capacity to ask other questions and can thus prevent you from being able to offer other critical or interesting stories or information. Whether you choose to employ mbaMission for a mock interview or practice in a mirror, we strongly recommend that you practice vocalizing your responses and not just writing them out on paper. Further, we suggest that you use a timer to get a sense of how long it takes you to answer each practice question—you would be surprised at how quickly two minutes can go by.

## Conversation, Not Memorization

Do not memorize or overplan your responses. Your goal is to be conversational, not robotic. Questions can come in many forms, and candidates who memorize potential answers tend to have trouble adjusting to questions that are asked in a new, different or otherwise unexpected way. In our experience, this is particularly relevant for open-ended questions like "Walk me through your resume" or "Tell me about yourself."

## Viewing a Story Through a Different Lens

While we do not recommend memorizing your responses, we do suggest developing a mental list of stories that you feel are important for you to tell. Try to incorporate your strongest stories/strengths into your interview at some point. If, for example, your experience as a youth soccer coach is an important story for you, you could work it into the interview as an example of leadership, teamwork, etc. when such a question is asked or these topics are raised. Your stories are far more flexible than you might realize and can be "spun" if need be.

Think of five to six key points (activities, personality traits, etc.) you absolutely want to be sure you get across during the interview. Then think about possible questions to which you can "hook" those points. For example, if you spend one afternoon a week tutoring inmates for their GED, potential "hook" questions for this activity could be as follows:

- Tell me about a time when you demonstrated initiative.

Example: *"I wanted to make a difference but wanted to move beyond just helping high school students. So I researched where in my area the biggest need was and found a program that brings volunteers to prisons to ... ."*

- Tell me about a time when you went above and beyond.

Example: *"For the past few years, I have been engaged in some meaningful service—teaching GED prep in a local prison. I was surprised to find that inmates were only allowed to attend one hour of extra tutoring per week. Recognizing that my students needed additional help, I devoted extensive time and effort to develop a series of math and vocabulary flash cards for them to use in between sessions. My additional efforts showed them that I truly was committed to their success. Further, the students found them to be extremely helpful—all five of them passed the GED that year!"*

- Tell me about a time when you had to motivate a reluctant person.

Example: *"My best example I believe occurred outside the office, as part of my volunteer work with inmates studying for their GED. Although most of the inmates I tutor are very motivated, once in a while I work with someone who … ."*

- What do you think you could bring to campus?

Example: *"With the inmates I tutor on a volunteer basis, I have to break down complex concepts into simple terms, and I believe I've become quite good at doing this. I believe at XYZ School, I could help my fellow classmates struggling in certain classes by taking this same approach."*

We must clarify, however, that we are *not* suggesting that you answer four different questions with the same story, but are merely attempting to illustrate how one important story can be "flexible." By selecting several key personal stories and examining them from several angles before your interview, you can better ensure that you will find a way to share them during your interview.

# Frequently Asked Questions

1. *Does a school-initiated interview (i.e., invitation) carry more weight than an applicant-initiated interview?* No, schools consider both options equal.

However, when a school offers the option of scheduling an interview, we recommend that you reserve a spot on its interview calendar as soon as possible. In particularly competitive years, interview slots can fill up quickly, and you do not want to miss out on a chance to interview!

2. *Does it matter if I travel to campus to interview or meet with a local alumnus/alumna to do so?* An on-campus interview and an interview with a graduate of the school in your area carry the same weight. However, we recommend that applicants who have not yet visited their target school and do not live overseas use the interview as an opportunity—if at all possible—to go to campus, attend a class and perhaps meet and/or have lunch with a student.

3. *What should I wear?* Always follow any guidelines the school provides on proper interview dress. If "business casual" is specified, wear business casual; if "business attire," dress in business attire. Jeans, T-shirts and ripped or unclean clothing are never appropriate. If the school does not specify a dress code, wear business attire for any on-campus interviews as well as for an off-campus interview with a member of the admissions staff. Business casual is often best when meeting an alumnus/alumna off campus, though you may consider politely asking the person you are meeting about proper attire in advance. Showing some creativity and style with your clothing is okay, but do not go overboard—remember that your meeting is essentially a professional one, and you want to make a good impression.

4. *I am meeting my interviewer at a coffee shop. Who pays?* If you are meeting an alumnus/alumna at a café or similar establishment for an interview, you can avoid the awkward "who pays?" scenario by arriving a few minutes early, purchasing your own beverage and then offering to pay for the interviewer's selection when he/she arrives. If your interviewer arrives before you, you might politely offer to pay for his/her drink, but if the interviewer declines, you should not insist.

5. *Should I send a thank you note?* Yes, you should always send a brief thank you note after your interview. Write and send the note as soon as possible after the interview—the same day or the next day is ideal—and be sure to mention specifics from your conversation or your visit. Emailing the thank you is fine. Interviewers usually need to submit their feedback on candidates within 24 hours, so you want your message to be received within this time frame.

These are only general rules. Our mbaMission consultants can provide additional guidance and personalized support with interview preparation, including conducting mock interviews and giving targeted feedback, as well as helping you formulate appropriate questions for the interviewer.

Interview

# Typical MBA Candidate Interview Questions

## General Introductory Questions:

*1.* Tell me about yourself.

*2.* Walk me through your resume. Briefly explain your roles/responsibilities in each of your positions and the specific dates of these positions.

*3.* Discuss your career progress since your graduation from college.

*4.* Tell me about your parents and family. Where do you come from?

*5.* Tell me about your life.

*6.* Tell me about your career.

*7.* What are your short-term and long-term career goals?

*8.* In what positions do you see yourself right after graduation and five years later?

9. Walk me through your career goals.

10. Why do you want/need an MBA to achieve your goals?

11. Why our MBA program?

**Career** (for simplicity's sake, some of the questions in this section assume the candidate's career goals involve being a consultant, but they can easily be adapted for any candidate's career goals):

12. What is general management?

13. What does a consultant do?

14. Why do you want to be a consultant?

15. What will you get out of your consulting experience? How will this help you reach the next stage of your career?

16. Can you be specific in defining your post-MBA career objectives?

17. Can you be specific in describing your goals as a consultant?

18. What skills do you have that will enable you to excel in this role?

19. What challenges do you anticipate in your career?

20. Aside from earning your MBA, how will you prepare for this career?

21. What skills will you gain from an MBA that will enable you to excel in this role?

22. Why do you need an MBA? Could you continue with your existing job and still achieve your goals?

23. How, specifically, can our program help you with your long-term goals?

24. What motivates you?

25. What will you if you do not get into an MBA program this year?

## Professional Experience:

26. What do you do exactly in your position?

27. Walk me through your responsibilities in your current position.

28. What do you like the most about your current job?

29. What do you like the least about your current job?

30. What do you find meaningful about your current position?

31. Describe a success and a failure you have experienced in your current position.

32. Tell me about a time you had to work with someone with whom you did not get along. Tell me more about the actual confrontation and how you handled it.

33. How do you manage your boss?

34. How have you taught those who are junior to you?

35. What accomplishment on your resume are you most proud of?

36. What is the current status of your company? What will happen to or within the company if you pursue your MBA? (for entrepreneurs, in particular)

37. Did you have opportunities to work for other companies after college? If so, why did you choose to accept a position at your current company?

38. XYZ must be great company to work for. What do you like about it?

Interview

39. Tell me about something from your current job that occurred within the past few months that most intrigued you.

40. Tell me about a professional regret or mistake.

41. How will you continue learning in your next position?

## Leadership/Teamwork:

42. What do you think are the qualities of a leader? Tell me about a time you displayed leadership.

43. What do you think are the most important elements of a high-performing team?

44. What do you think it is about your personality that gives you the ability to interact with diverse types of people, business partners, etc.?

45. Discuss an example of when you displayed leadership. How were you a successful leader?

46. Why makes you good at your job? What are your strengths?

47. What makes a great leader, and what characteristics must a leader project to employees to be effective?

48. How do you think you can have an impact on a team/business without holding a leadership role? Give an example of a time when you made a difference in such a non-leadership role.

49. Recall a specific time when you encountered team conflicts (i.e., conflicts among individuals within a team). What did you do to resolve the conflict?

50. How do you function in a team?

51. How do you lead a group?

52. Pick two words that would describe what you would not do in a team setting.

53. If you did not agree with a team member, how would you approach the situation?

54. If you had a team member who was contributing less than other team members, what would you do to motivate him or her?

55. What is your definition of leadership? Relate it to a leadership experience.

56. What would your current teammates say about you, and would you agree with their assessment?

57. What kind of relationship do you have with your managers? Do you always agree?

58. Please provide an example from work when you were asked to come up with an innovative idea. What were the results?

59. What characteristics do you think a good leader should have?

60. Tell me about a leader you admire and why.

61. How would your subordinates describe you?

62. What skills would you bring to a learning team or study group?

63. Discuss an ethical challenge that you have faced at the office.

64. Tell me about a time when you disagreed with your manager. How did you manage your relationship? What were the implications?

65. How and when do you seek the advice of others?

66. How would you describe your risk tolerance?

## Personal:

*67.* You have made many decisions, both large and small, in your life. If you could change one decision, what would it be and why?

*68.* Going from working to studying is a big change. How will you prepare yourself, or how have you already prepared yourself?

*69.* How would your friends describe you?

*70.* In what extracurricular activities were you involved during college?

*71.* What was your most difficult personal hurdle, and how did you overcome it?

*72.* What are three principles that you hold dear and why?

*73.* Why did you choose your undergraduate program?

*74.* Would you do anything differently in your undergraduate studies if given the opportunity?

*75.* What is unique about you?

*76.* What else would you like to tell me about you?

*77.* What will you do if you are not accepted into our school?

*78.* What is the last book you read?

*79.* What global issue is most important to you?

*80.* Where have you traveled?

*81.* How do you connect with others when you travel?

## Specific to the School:

82. What specifically about our program attracted you to it?

83. How did you learn about our program?

84. Have you visited our classrooms? If so, what did you think?

85. Have you spoken to any of our current students or to any alumni?

86. If you were accepted, which extracurricular activities would you participate in?

87. If you were accepted, which country would you choose to study in/visit and why?

88. What concerns do you have about attending our school?

89. Why us? Please do not tell me the typical reasons that every candidate cites.

90. What unique contribution will you make in our classroom?

91. What unique contributions will you make in our social/cultural environment?

92. To which other schools have you applied?

93. What aspect of your application worries you the most?

94. What do you believe is the greatest strength of your candidacy? Weakness?

95. If you came back to this school in 15 years for a class reunion, what would your classmates remember about you?

Interview

96. What will be the key difference between your life now and your life when you are a student at our school?

## Final Questions from the Interviewer:

97. If you had one minute to directly address the admissions committee, what would you say?

98. Would you like to discuss anything specific in your application?

99. Do you have any questions for me?

100. What else would you like the admissions committee to know about you?

# Waitlist

Chapter 9

# *Waitlist*

"You have been placed on the waitlist."

In some ways, those seven words are more dreaded by business school candidates than a straightforward rejection, because spending time on a school's waitlist means that the agony of waiting for a decision is prolonged indefinitely. Admissions committees rarely indicate when they believe a final decision will be rendered, so you just might remain in admissions purgatory for months. Still, as frustrating as this situation can be, there is hope. Although being placed on the waitlist is certainly not as satisfying as being accepted, it does mean that the admissions committee likes what it sees and does not want to lose the opportunity to have you in the school's next class. Indeed, admissions committees have waitlists so that they can maintain the option of accepting certain candidates in the future as the incoming class starts to take shape—not to torment innocent applicants. So, if you find yourself on your target school's waitlist, do your best to see the glass as half full, as they say.

Unfortunately, waitlist processes tend to be pretty opaque. Most top schools are loathe to release information regarding the number of applicants on their waitlist and the number of candidates they expect to ultimately accept from that list, for fear that waitlisted applicants will either lose interest or give up and make other plans. Further, virtually all schools state that they do not rank waitlist applicants; this seems logical, given that the school wants the right to continuously evaluate candidates against others in the incoming class and to make their admissions decisions as the incoming class takes shape.

In addition, schools will often give very broad time frames for when a decision will be made, and some offer only a date by which an applicant will receive a final decision, which can be as late as the first day of classes. Typically, schools will slowly release decisions over several months. Most schools release FAQs about their waitlist process, and if your target school provides such information, it will be included in the decision email they send to applicants. This brings us to the most important rule of waitlist etiquette: *Listen to the admissions committee.*

If the admissions committee tells you *not* to send follow-up material of any sort, do not yield to temptation and send files or other items that you think will bolster your case and give you an advantage over your silent (or so you believe) peers. If you *do* (misguidedly) choose to provide the school with additional information about your candidacy when the admissions committee has specifically requested that you *not*, you will only succeed in identifying yourself in a negative way. This is most definitely *not* the kind of message you want to send to a group that will be determining your fate.

An example of a *closed* waitlist process, in which the candidate is asked *not* to send follow-up material, is the University of Pennsylvania's Wharton. A sample of a Wharton waitlist decision correspondence follows:

*Thank you for your application to the Wharton MBA program. After a careful review of your application materials, the Admissions Committee has decided to place you on the waitlist at this time. We recognize that this news likely brings with it mixed emotions, but we hope that among these is a sense of pride at being recognized—from a pool of exceptionally talented candidates—as someone who has outstanding potential to contribute to the Wharton community.*

*Should you wish to withdraw your application, please send an e-mail to mbaoperations@wharton.upenn.edu with the subject header "Waitlist Remove."*

*In the spirit of fairness and equity toward all candidates, we will not accept additional materials for inclusion in your application. Thank you in advance for honoring this policy.*

*We greatly appreciate the time and energy you put into applying to the Wharton MBA Program. We look forward to reconsidering your application in the coming months.*

*Sincerely,*
*J.J. Cutler, WG '97*
*Director*

What is interesting about Wharton's waitlist notification is that the school does not even ask candidates to confirm whether they would like to remain on the waitlist, instead asking only that they inform the school if they would like to be removed from the list. In mbaMission's exclusive interview with J.J. Cutler, Wharton's director of admissions and financial aid, in January of 2010, we specifically asked him how serious he was about limiting correspondence from waitlisted applicants:

*mbaMission: Another thing you've been very clear about on your blog is that you don't want to hear from people on the waitlist. But candidates seem to believe that there's some trickery in this, that they can beat down your door in some way, and that this is some sort of test. So can you be unequivocal both in terms of candidate communication and third-party communication about candidates who are on the waitlist?*

*JJC: Sure. The first thing I'd say is, if you're on the waitlist, that isn't necessarily a bad thing. I mean, by definition it means you are admissible. It means you are quite competitive, and it means you're sort of still "in the mix." Right?... It's just that we need a little bit more time to see a few more different things, mostly things that are outside the applicant's control, before we can make a final decision one way or the other.*

*So the first point is, we're very serious when we say we don't want people to contact us. It's not a joke. It's not a test. It's not a trick. We really don't want to hear anything else. And there are really a couple of reasons for*

Waitlist

*that. One is we want to be fair to everyone. Two is the factors we're wait-*
*ing for have nothing to do with the applicant at that point. They've put*
*their application together, like everybody else, and we are unable yet to*
*make a final decision on their application. And that's almost all about*
*not yet having enough information about things external to the applica-*
*tion. So more information about the applicant isn't what's causing our*
*decision not to yet be made. It's that we need more time to see what hap-*
*pens with other things that are outside the application. And that can be*
*around class size. It can be that we need to see what the next round looks*
*like. It could be that we need to see what decisions are made by other*
*applicants.*

*So, we really don't want more information. It wouldn't be fair—we don't*
*want to allow people to reopen and resubmit materials unless we do that*
*for everybody. And we really don't need any more information at that*
*point. We've decided that you are admissible; we just need a little bit more*
*time to get a little more information before we can make a final decision.*
*And so that's how I would characterize the waitlist situation.*

Similar to Wharton, Harvard Business School (HBS) has a closed waitlist
policy and is serious about maintaining a level playing field. On its Web site
(www.hbs.edu/mba/admissions/waitlist/index.html), the HBS admissions
committee offers a waitlist FAQ, which includes the following information:

*HBS waitlist policies differ from those at most other MBA programs. We*
*request that you not send additional materials, nor can we accommodate*
*requests for meetings or interviews.*

*HBS is fully committed to the online application process. We cannot*
*consider materials submitted outside the online application. This*
*includes recommendations: additional letters of recommendation cannot*
*be considered once your application has been submitted.*

*We are also committed to fair and equitable consideration of all candidates. For this reason, we must reinforce our by-invitation-only interview process.*

Unlike Wharton and HBS, some schools have an *open* waitlist policy, meaning that they will permit waitlisted candidates to follow up with a personal update letter or relevant information (e.g., test scores, new grades). The University of California Berkeley's Haas, Duke University's Fuqua and the University of Michigan's Ross are a few such schools. A sample waitlist letter from Berkeley Haas follows:

*Your application for admission to the Berkeley MBA Program is being held for further consideration. While we find your strengths and accomplishments more impressive than the majority of our applicants, the highly competitive nature of our admission process is such that we are unable to offer admission to more than a small percentage of our applicants at this time.*

*We would like to continue your candidacy by offering you a place on the waitlist. As a waitlisted candidate, you are able to submit additional materials for your application, provided that these materials add new information.*

*There are many things that you can do to enhance your candidacy:*

*1) We strongly encourage you to schedule an interview if you have not already had one as a part of the admissions process. In addition to interviewing on campus, you may also schedule an interview in other cities around the US and the world. To request an interview, please use the Interview Scheduler link available on the Status Report page of your online application. (NOTE: You will not be able to schedule an interview until you first accept a place on our waitlist by following the directions below.)*

Waitlist

*2) If your GMAT or TOEFL scores fall below our averages, you may wish to retake the test and forward an unofficial score (followed by your official score) to the admissions office.*

*3) If you feel you have not sufficiently demonstrated quantitative ability to the Admissions Committee, as shown by your undergraduate and graduate level coursework and by the quantitative subscore on the GMAT, you may wish to enroll in a statistics or calculus course at a local college, retake the GMAT, or do both.*

*4) You may provide an additional letter of recommendation (or two) to your file, if the letter will add information that was not provided in the original letters submitted. New letters may be submitted in hard copy or electronically. To request a new online recommendation, you must enter the Recommendations section of your online application and provide the requested information regarding your new recommender. (NOTE: You will not be able to request a new online recommendation until you first accept a place on our waitlist by following the directions below.)*

*5) You may submit a new statement (via mail, fax, or email) updating the Admissions Committee on any relevant changes in your professional or personal life since your application was submitted.*

*6) You should check your status on-line https://ssl.haas.berkeley.edu/Admissions/status/ to see if there are additional materials needed before a final decision can be made on your application. If so, now is the time for you to provide those materials to the Admissions Office.*

*Please note that we do not rank our waitlist. We periodically review all waitlisted candidates, so you may receive a final decision from us as early as one month from now or as late as August. While we regret that we cannot be more encouraging at this time, please be assured that only a highly select group of qualified applicants is offered a place on our waitlist.*

*To accept a place on the waitlist, please respond to this email as soon as possible. If we do not hear from you by Friday, February 5, we will assume that you are no longer interested in being considered for admission, and your application will be withdrawn. As noted above, you will not be able to schedule an interview or request a new online recommendation until you accept a place on the waitlist. After we receive your response, it will take us one business day to update our database so that you can schedule your interview and/or request your new online recommendation.*

*We appreciate your interest in the Berkeley MBA and your patience with the application process. If you have any questions, please feel free to contact the admissions office directly at 510-642-XXXX.*

*Sincerely,*
*—The Berkeley MBA Admissions Committee*

So, when you are dealing with an *open* waitlist, you can rejoice in feeling that you can still influence the committee positively. However, a new worry may materialize: "What can I offer the MBA admissions committee as an update when I just submitted my application three months ago?!"

Many candidates are dismissive of updating the committee with qualitative information, but such data can be quite useful in painting a picture of your continued growth and progress. If you have undertaken any additional networking or have completed a class visit since submitting your application, you can offer a new window into your ever-growing interest in the school. (When you are on a waitlist, the MBA admissions committee wants to know that you are passionately committed to the school.) Further, even if you have not been promoted, you can creatively reflect on a project that you have started since the application deadline and identify the new professional skills/exposure that this project has provided, such as managing people off-site for the first time or executing certain responsibilities with greater independence. Finally, the personal realm is usually not "off limits," so you should also feel

Waitlist

free to discuss any non-work-related accomplishments, from advancing in your study of a language to visiting a new country to completing a triathlon, for example.

Of course, you can offer quantifiable results as well, such as having retaken the GMAT and increased your score. If you find yourself on a school's wait-list, take a moment to pause and reflect on your GMAT scores and your academic performance: have you truly proven your quantitative and analytical abilities? If you have a weakness in these areas—a poor grade in calculus in college or a 60th percentile on the quantitative section of the GMAT, for example—taking steps to improve in these areas, such as reattempting the GMAT or taking a supplemental math class, could help you prove to the admissions committee that you truly possess those skills that may otherwise be in doubt. Please note, however, that we are not suggesting that you rush to take the GMAT again as a kind of "knee-jerk" reaction, but if you feel that you still have room to improve and will likely better your score should you take the exam again, then you should consider doing so. Earning and submitting an improved GMAT score while on the waitlist could help you, though it is not the "ticket" to a guaranteed acceptance—just one piece of the puzzle.

Further, if you have concrete news regarding a promotion in your professional life or if you have assumed additional responsibilities in your community, you should definitely update the MBA admissions committee on this. A promotion is a quantifiable event and can really only be interpreted one way—positively. Likewise, taking a leadership position by directing a community project or joining the board of an organization highlights your commitment and initiative.

If you have additional letters of recommendation that add a *new* window into your candidacy—and, of course, if the school is open to receiving additional letters—you should send one (two at the most). However, you should refrain from sending a repetitive letter—one that offers no new information about your experience, personality or abilities—just to feel that you are sending something. Exercise judgment when considering whether to send additional letters. Ask yourself, "Is there someone out there who has something interesting and different to say about me—something fresh?" If you originally submitted two work recommendations and have another supervisor who is willing to write for you, his/her recommendation probably won't do anything to advance your candidacy. However, if you work closely with someone through your volunteer activities who would be open to writing a letter on your behalf, for example, this might be a good option to consider.

We do want to sound a cautionary note. If you decide to send additional information, you should be thoughtful and sparing and take care to strictly follow the advice of the admissions committees (the Berkeley letter, for example, is explicit in its directions). Ask yourself a simple question: "Is this information I would want to receive if I were evaluating a candidate, or is this just correspondence for its own sake?" We recommend fewer interactions, and only those that indeed count. In other words, do not flood the admissions committee with additional information. Your target school may be open to receiving new information, but it is not seeking a constant flow. Persistent emails, constant additional letters of support and expressions of anxiety about the process are all negatives. Indeed—and we cannot be explicit enough on this point—resist any temptation to call the school and ask about your status. Repeated calls will only identify you as a nuisance!

Do not interpret a lack of movement on the waitlist to mean a lack of interest on your target school's behalf; the MBA program has many candidates—and many outside factors—to constantly reevaluate. The waitlist is not a joke—you are on it because the school might just want to accept you. Unfortunately, being on the waitlist is akin to running a marathon, not a 100 meter dash. You will need to stay in the race for the long haul, hoping to eventually top many talented competitors (and most schools will update you about cuts to the list).

Waitlist

With a patient approach, complemented by some thought and creativity, you should be able to develop concise and powerful communications with the admissions committee at your target schools. By showing your continued professional and personal growth, while also expressing your sincere and ever-growing interest in the school, you should increase your chances of ultimately gaining admission.

# Sample Letter A: Open Waitlist

*Dear Mr. Stevens,[1]*

*Since receiving my waitlist decision one month ago, I have determinedly continued to learn more about the ABC School to be best prepared to join the class, should the opportunity arise. Last week, I visited the ABC campus, eager to experience a case discussion firsthand. I admittedly did not expect the manic energy and humor that Professor Paul Johnson brought to the "Finance II" class, but amid his sprints to the board and rapid-fire questioning of the unsuspecting, I learned a profound lesson on the connection between inventory management and working capital needs. I was sold on the case method before my visit, but my experience with the Clarkson Lumber case only reinforced that this is the ideal, active learning style for me. I should add that I was fortunate to join the learning team of my former colleague Akira Frances (a fellow McKinley alumnus) that evening and observed the team dissect the next day's cases. Seeing her engaged in such a collaborative learning environment made me certain that I would be a solid fit both academically and socially.[2]*

*When I submitted my application, I was about to begin a new case at McKinley. Today, three months later, this project is quickly moving forward. At McKinley, I previously worked exclusively on due diligence assessments for private equity firms; I recently asked to join a strategic re-*

Waitlist

---

1   This is the name of the waitlist manager assigned to the waitlisted student.
2   By including details about his school visit, the candidate shows commitment to and fit with the target program.

*view and am now evaluating potential divestitures for a media firm. As I study this firm, I find that I am fascinated by the mix of old media and new media assets and by the nebulous nature of making decisions on assets whose prices seem to change each day. I have twice met with the firm's CFO and its VP for Strategic Planning, and we have now determined which assets are "non-core" and are considering options, including selling such expendable assets to competitors or to one of the private equity firms for which I completed a due diligence project. In fact, I was quite proud to have made the introduction myself.[3] This new experience has been invigorating and has only reinforced my desire to return to McKinley after completing my MBA,[4] as discussed in depth in my personal statement.*

*Despite my busy schedule, I remain committed to the Golden Heights Senior Center, where I lead Bingo each Sunday and play in the "house band" each Wednesday night. Last month, instead of leading both activities, I organized a weekend trip for 20 seniors to the Super Casino and arranged to play Bingo there and attend an instrumental show with an acoustic Beatles tribute band.[5] Needless to write, perhaps, it was an experience that none of us will forget.*

*I remain committed to attending the ABC School next year[6] and am optimistic that I will find a place in your class. I will continue to apprise the admissions committee of my progress and remain available should you have any questions at all.*

*Sincerely,*
*Aaron Goldstein*

Waitlist

---

3   This text offers some new information about the candidate's current job, but it is not revolutionary. Although he has not received a promotion, he has been enjoying a new experience and new responsibilities at work, and his description of this experience provides a sense of the candidate's growth.

4   The applicant confirms his career goals here and reminds the school about his plans to rejoin McKinley after graduating.

5   Here the candidate reminds the reader of his outside interests and reinforces his sense of humor, humility, dedication and entrepreneurship.

6   The candidate reiterates his interest in the school.

# Sample Letter B: Open Waitlist

*Dear Mr. Stevens,[1]*

*Following up on my update of March 1, 2010, I am writing briefly to notify the admissions committee of two material changes in my candidacy. First, two weeks ago, I completed my "Calculus I" and "Statistics I" classes at the ABC University Extension School, and yesterday morning, my professors informed me that I earned As[2] in both of their classes. Even though I work in a highly analytical capacity at McKinley, as a liberal arts major, I felt it important to clearly establish my quantitative competencies and I am hoping that my As in these recent courses will enable me to do so.*

*Second, I am excited to report that I took the GMAT for a second time and earned a slightly higher score, a 710.[3] What is noteworthy is that my quantitative score rose from a 75th percentile to an 85th percentile—which I believe serves as further proof of my quant skills and my ability to make contributions in this area. I will follow up shortly by sending my official GMAT score report and my transcripts for these classes.*

*Moreover, I have continued my networking[4] and recently had lunch with Fred Jones, ABC MBA '67, who is a partner at McKinley. I was impressed that Mr. Jones is still active with the alumni association and in touch with, by his estimation, no less than 30 members of his class of 240, all these years later. In addition to my belief in the case study, I feel that working closely with my peers and developing enduring relationships is very important. I saw this on display when I visited a class and*

---

1 The waitlisted candidate later sends a second letter to his waitlist manager to provide additional relevant information.

2 The applicant informs the committee of a very clear and material change in his candidacy and also reminds the committee that he is mitigating his potential perceived weakness due to his liberal arts background.

3 Again, the writer informs the committee of a material change in his candidacy and reinforces that he has the quantitative skills necessary to succeed in the program.

4 A subtle expression of interest—the candidate is clearly still doing his homework, and the admissions committee can thus be assured that he is still interested in this MBA program.

*a learning team meeting with Akira Frances last month, and Mr. Jones's enthusiasm for the school and anecdotes about his class only reinforced my feeling that ABC MBA is the ideal place for me to live and learn for two years and one I will continue to "experience" throughout my life.*

*I remain entirely committed to being a member of the ABC School class next year.*

*Sincerely,*
*Aaron Goldstein*

Waitlist

# Closing Thoughts

## Chapter 10

# *Closing Thoughts*

Over the years, I have personally conducted thousands of free one-on-one consultations and have spoken before thousands of MBA aspirants through the live and "live online" events that we host in different cities each month (http://www.mbamission.com/blog/category/mbamission-events/). At the end of these sessions and events, the most common question that I am asked by MBA candidates is a version of the following:

> *"What is the one secret that you can share with me that will get me into my target school?"*

Let me start to respond to this question with a brief digression. I have been in the admissions consulting business for more than ten years and I have met with the admissions officers from virtually all of the top schools. Each time I encounter one, I say, "I tell candidates all the time that admissions is an art, not a science. I feel silly asking you this, but I want to be sure that I am telling my candidates the truth. Is there a formula for getting into your school?"

My question is always met with a chuckle. I can tell you unequivocally—directly from many admissions officers—that the MBA admissions process is not a code that you need to "crack" and that attempts to game the process or become something that you are not are futile. We offer the words of Derrick Bolton, assistant dean and director of admissions at the Stanford Graduate School of Business, who could not have said it better via his admissions office's Web page:

> *"Because we want to discover who you are, resist the urge to 'package' yourself in order to come across in a way you think Stanford wants. Such attempts simply blur our understanding of who you are and what you can accomplish. We want to hear your genuine voice throughout the essays that you write and this is the time to think carefully about your values, your passions, your hopes and dreams."*

Throughout this book, we have attempted to give you the tools, but certainly not a formula, to create a standout application and grab the attention of the admissions committee. Our approach is all about harnessing the inherent power of your own story. We encourage you to fully explore yourself via multi-dimensional brainstorming, write a clear narrative in your voice, create a resume that reveals consistent accomplishments and more. By doing so, you are not guaranteed to be accepted, but you will tell your best story, and that will give you your best shot at your top school. And that is what mbaMission is all about…

Sincerely,

Jeremy Shinewald